Zillas Ruining Classic Art

(and other atrocities)

by

damian willcox

"ZILLAS RUINING CLASSIC ART (AND OTHER ATROCITIES)"
© 2016 damian willcox
published by dorkboy comics in canada

www.dorkboycomics.com

short excerpts may be reproduced for review purposes.

contact: damian@dorkboycomics.com

'ZILLAS RUINING CLASSIC ART (AND OTHER ATROCITIES)' contains a number of works of parody. No endorsements by any company or person parodied is intended or inferred. The law regarding parody is based upon the "fair use" doctrine under the U.S. Copyright Act. Under this doctrine, certain uses of copyrighted works, which would otherwise be considered infringing, are permissible.

INTRODUCTION

I ran into a problem putting this book together this year...I actually had TOO MUCH material - even with making this book bigger than I had planned, I still had to leave out a number of pieces.

Last year I was focused on my 20th anniversary retrospective book collecting many of my older out of print comics. While I was also continuing to make new comics during that time they could not be included in that book and so here I am now with a lot of additional content for this book.

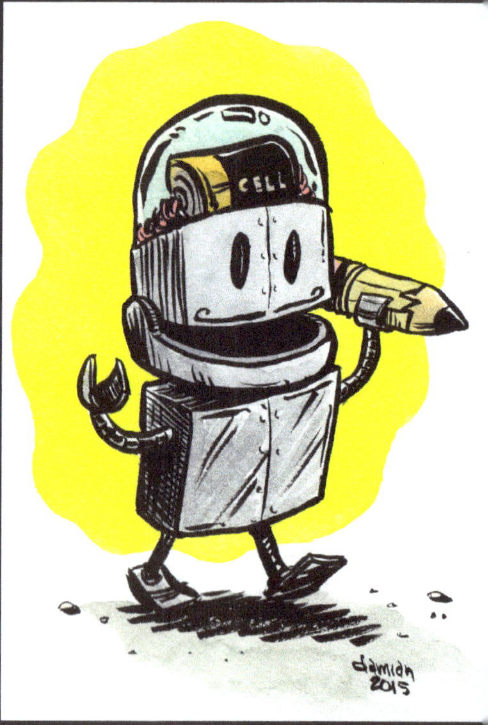
CELL
damian
2015

"let me pencil you in"

"i heard that sound"

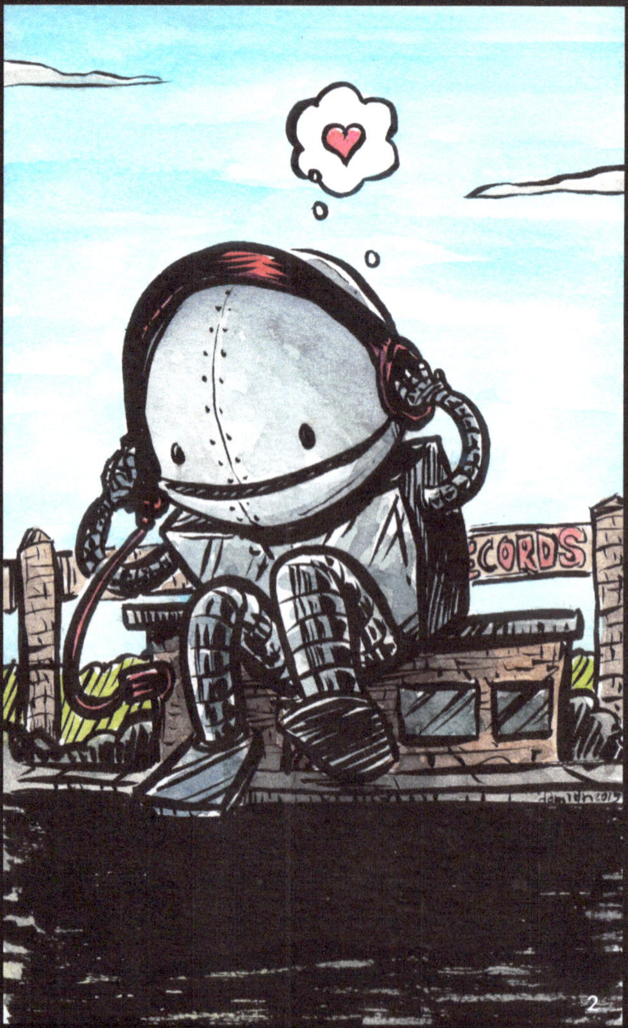
CORDS

That said, I have done my best to include as much work as I possibly could.

A smarter man may have held back artwork for the book they will need to make next year - but I am not that man. Of course, this simply means that I must continue to make comics and artwork in order to have work to include in my next book. Simply put, I have not allowed myself to be lazy, because the last thing you need to deal with is a lazy cartoonist. It's bad enough you have to deal with me and my silly doodlings.

Anyway, I truly hope you enjoy this new monster of a book!

your friendly neighbourhood cartoonist,

damian

ZILLAS RUINING CLASSIC ART

The following series began innocently enough, starting with a Zilla infiltrating the famed Mona Lisa, after which I continued on at a steady pace desecrating masterpiece after masterpiece - hopefully learning something in the process, but also enjoying the chance to mimic some favourites of mine such as Hokusai and M.C. Escher.

Learn about the amazing originals:
1. "The Scream" by Edvard Munch
2. "Mona Lisa" by Leonardo da Vinci
3. "Hand with Reflecting Sphere" by M.C. Escher
4. "The Runaway" by Norman Rockwell
5. "The Birth of Venus" by Sandro Botticelli
6. "The Creation of Adam" by Michelangelo
7. "Venus de Milo" by Alexandros of Antioch
8. "The Starry Night" by Vincent Van Gogh
9. "Nighthawks" by Edward Hopper
10. "The Great Wave off Kanagawa" by Katsushika Hokusai
11. "American Gothic" by Grant Wood
12. "A Friend in Need" by Cassius Marcellus Coolidge

For the last painting in this series, I wanted to do one of the most well known works of art by one of the least known artists. Cassius Marcellus Coolidge painted a series of paintings involving dogs playing pool, poker and more – none of them titled "dogs playing poker". The one I based this off of was actually titled "a friend in need".

I discovered that he and I have a couple of things in common – we both wrote a comic opera (King Gallinipper in his case, Too Much Coffee Man in mine), and neither of us attended art school...that's probably where the similarities end though. He was not solely a career painter – he had an interesting life holding various jobs and also founded the first bank and the first newspaper in his hometown. He also holds a patent as the inventor of comic foregrounds – those caricatured wooden panels of cartoon bodybuilders, swimsuit bodies, etc with an opening for your head that you take photos with at amusement parks.

His various "dogs" paintings were largely intended as reproduction art (similar to how comics are) and adorned cigar boxes and so on, as well as prints to be hung in homes everywhere. Read more about him at dogsplayingpoker.org.

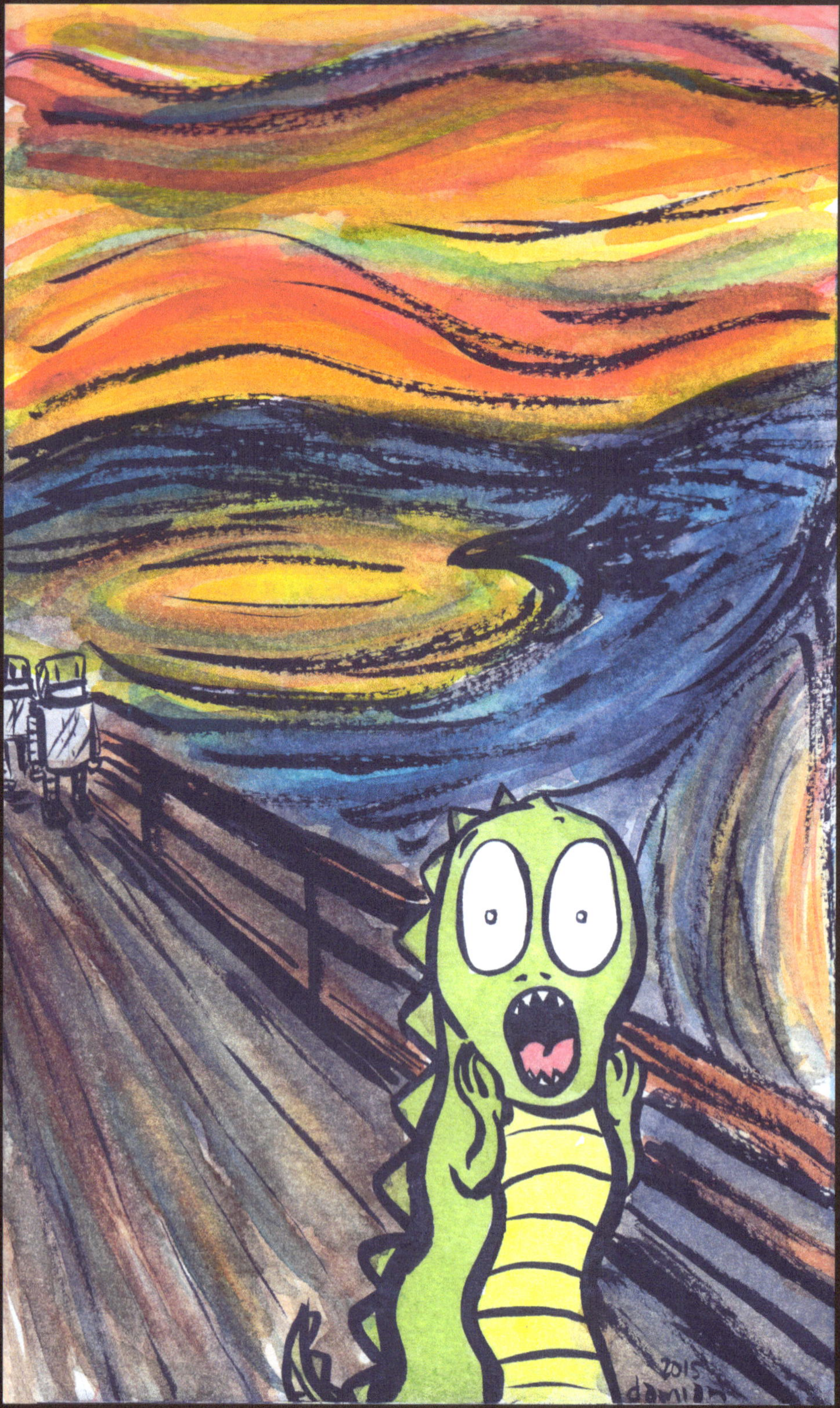

"The Scream(ing Zilla)"

(ink & watercolour)

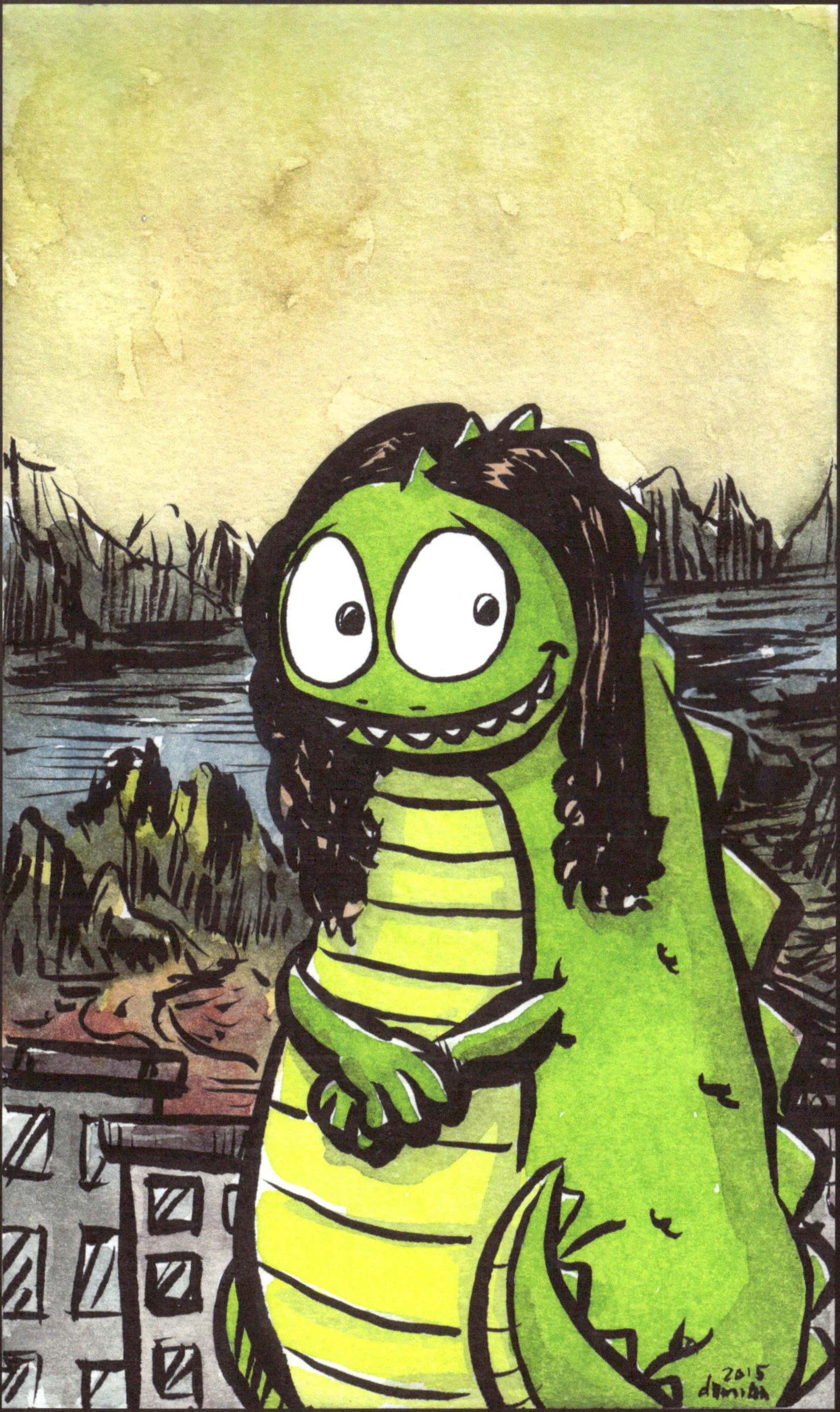
2015

"Mona Zilla"

(ink & watercolour)

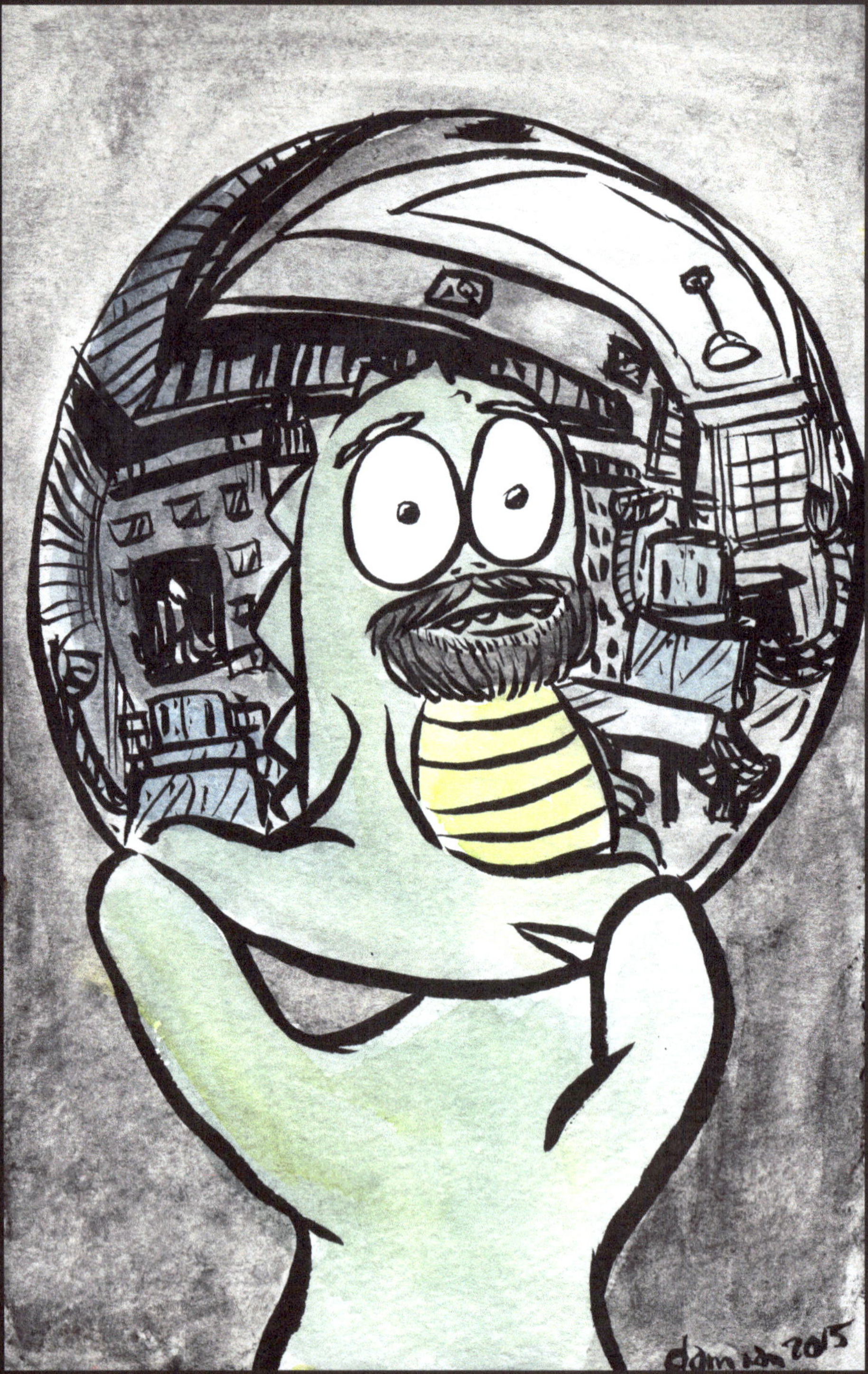
damian 2015

"Hand with Reflecting Zilla"

(ink & watercolour)

SPECIAL TODAY
Norman Rockzilla
damian 2015

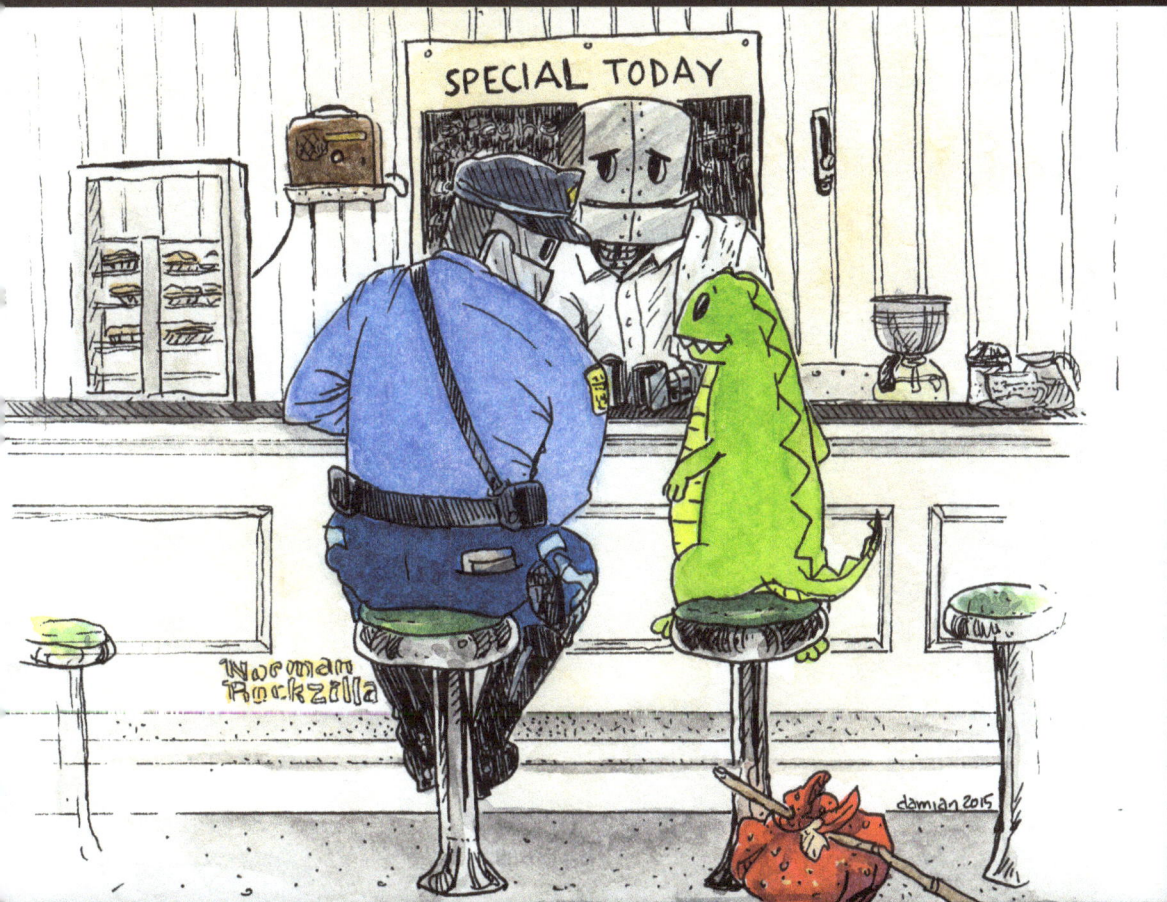

“The Runaway Zilla”

(ink & watercolour)

"The Birth of Venuszilla"

(ink & watercolour)

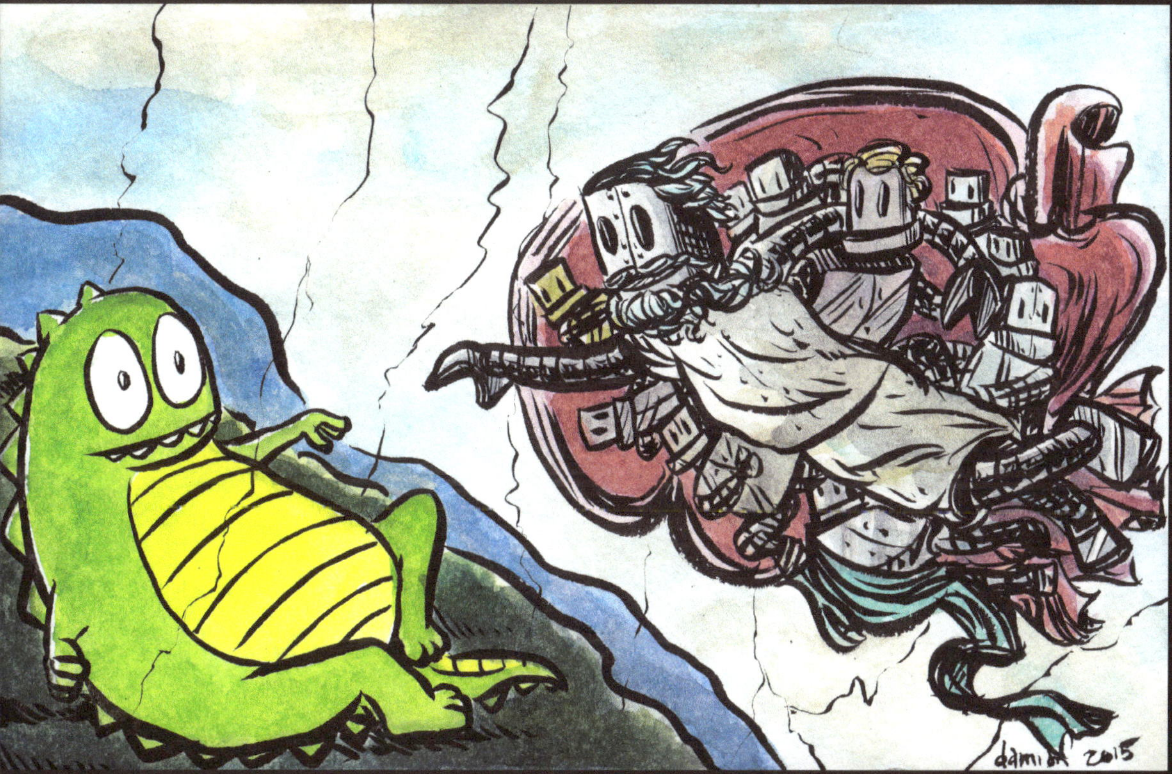
damian 2015

"The Creation of Zilla"

(ink & watercolour)

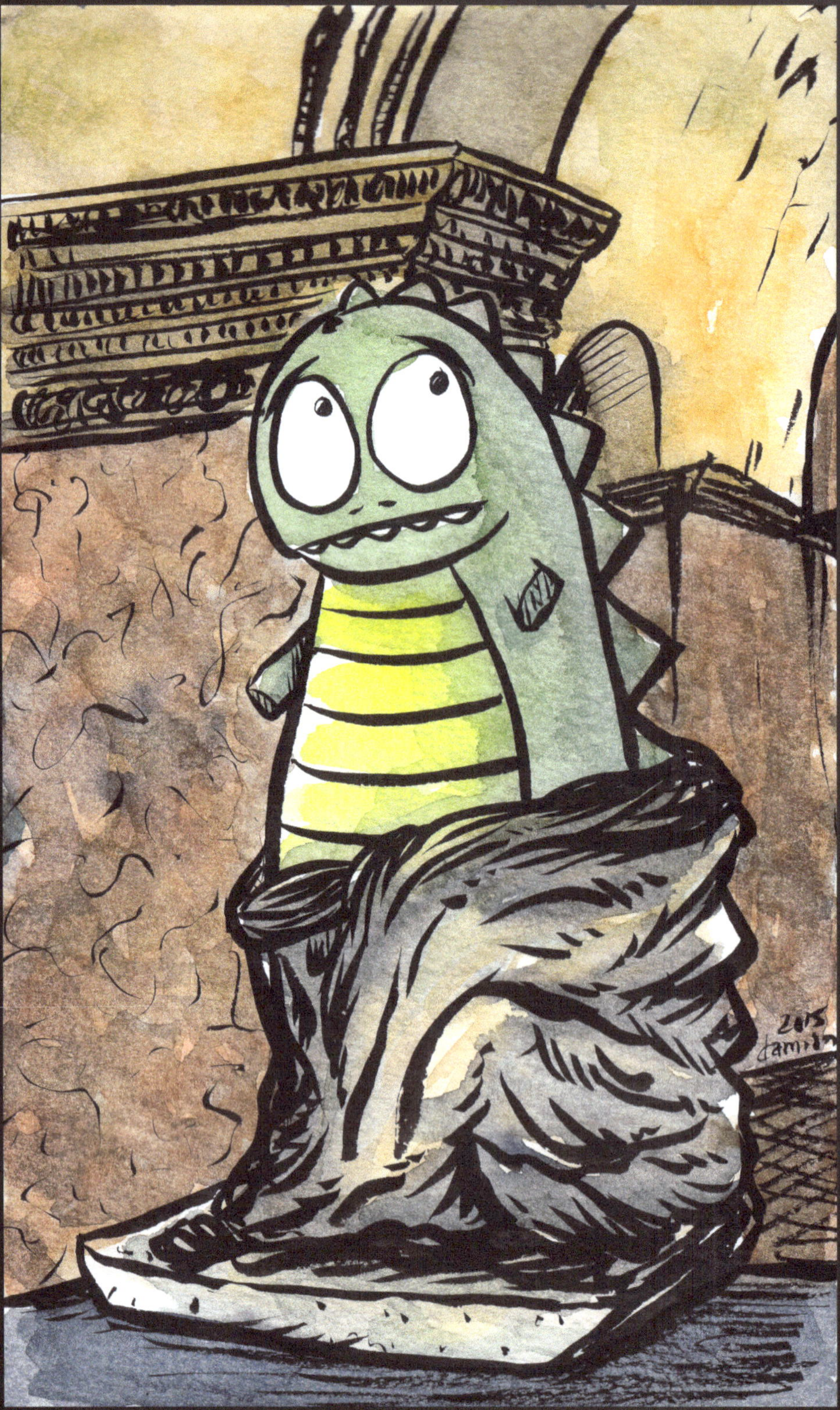

“Venus de Zillo”

(ink & watercolour)

"Starry Night (of Mayhem)"

(ink & watercolour)

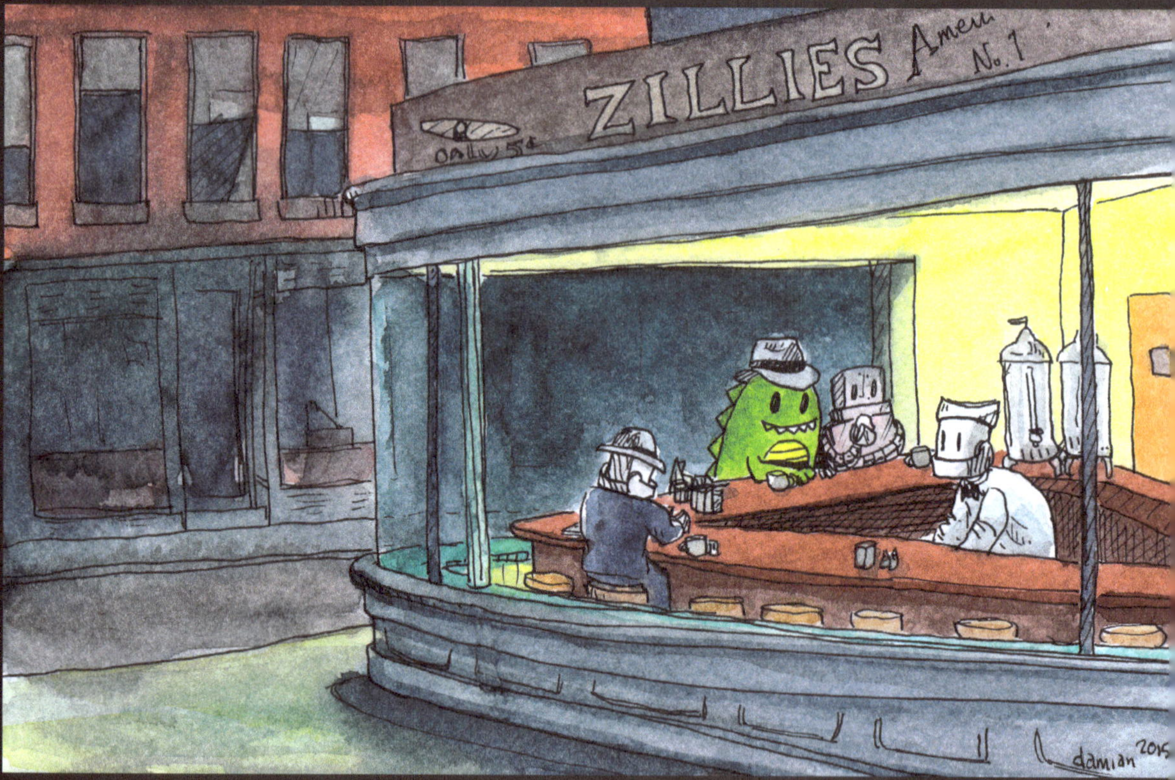
ZILLIES
N. 1
damian 2015

“Night Hawkz(illa)”

(ink & watercolour)

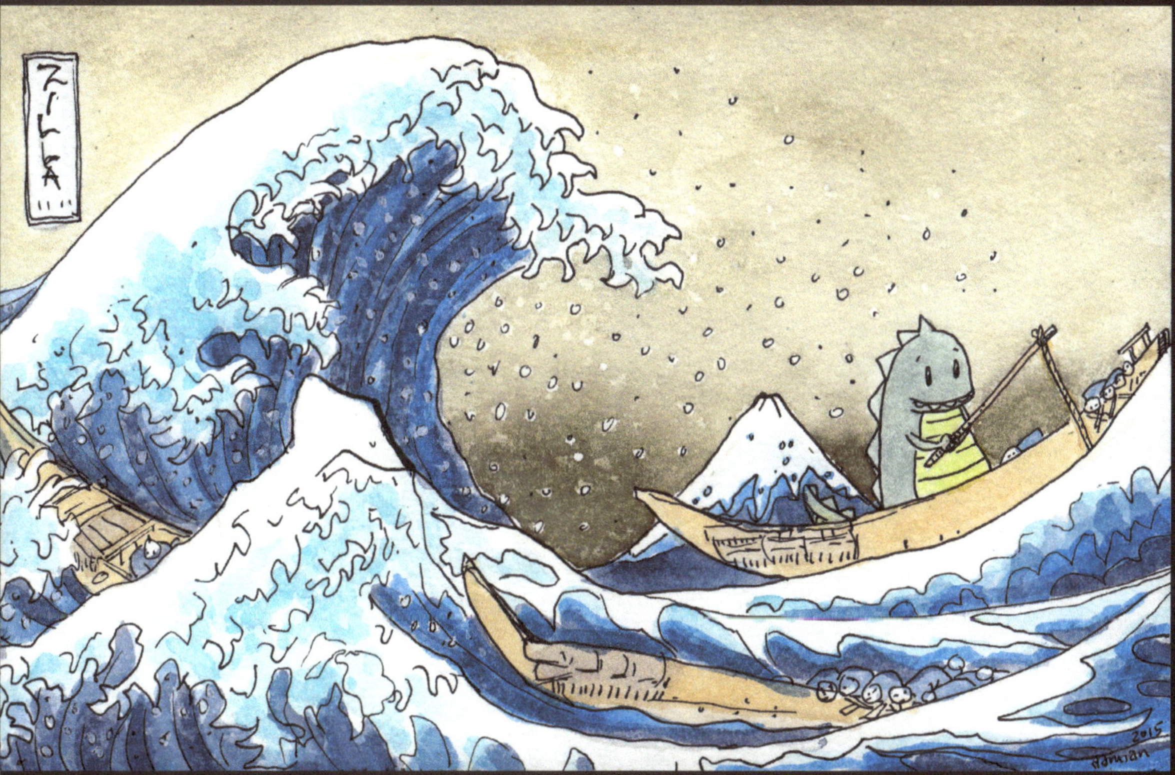
2015
damian

"Hokuzilla's Great Wave"

(ink & watercolour)

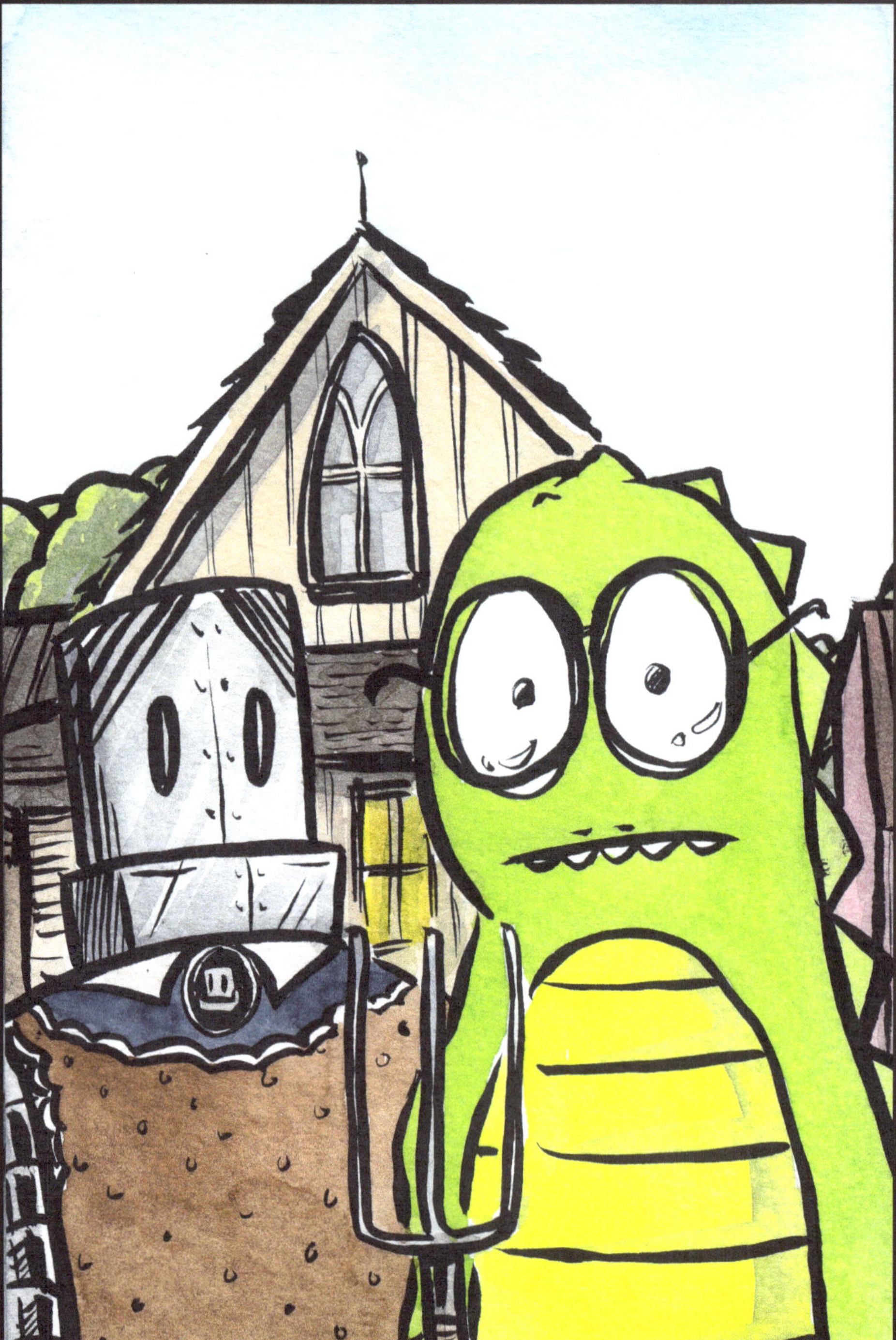
2015 damian

"American Godzic"

(ink & watercolour)

"A Zilla in Need"

(ink & watercolour)

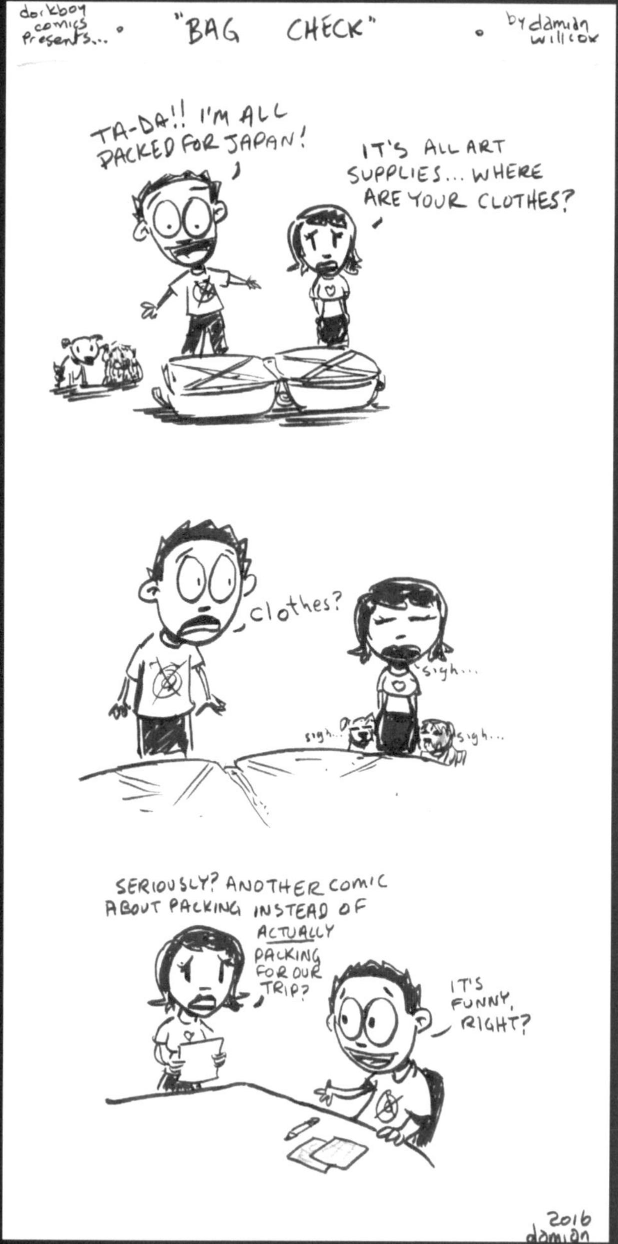
dorkboy comics presents...
"BAG CHECK"
by damian willcox
TA-DA!! I'M ALL PACKED FOR JAPAN!
IT'S ALL ART SUPPLIES... WHERE ARE YOUR CLOTHES?
clothes?
sigh...
sigh...
sigh...
SERIOUSLY? ANOTHER COMIC ABOUT PACKING INSTEAD OF ACTUALLY PACKING FOR OUR TRIP?
IT'S FUNNY, RIGHT?
2016 damian

I have really been enjoying making more spontaneous sketchbook comics recently - straight to ink, no penciling and no planning, just hope for the best and try to capture an idea as best I can with no recourse when mistakes happen. It helps me capture a lot more of my comic ideas, and most times I feel like they turn out better than ones that I spend too much time on or overthink. Here are a couple for you that coincide with the travel comic theme in this section...

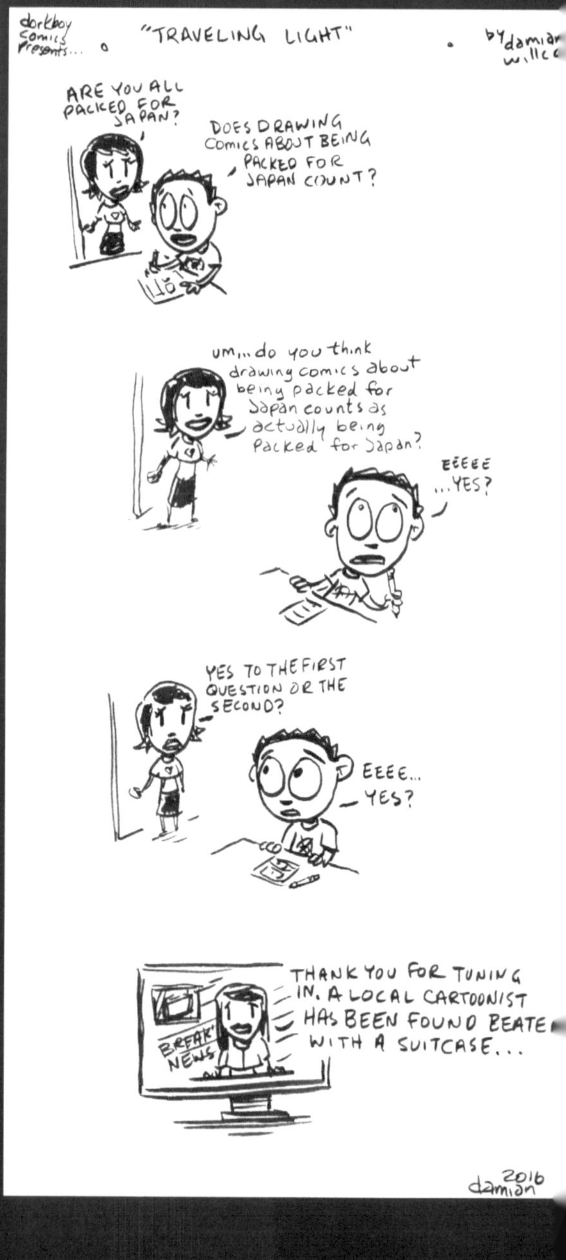
dorkboy comics presents...
"TRAVELING LIGHT"
by damia
ARE YOU ALL PACKED FOR JAPAN?
DOES DRAWING COMICS ABOUT BEING PACKED FOR JAPAN COUNT?
um... do you think drawing comics about being packed for Japan counts as actually being packed for Japan?
EEEEE ...YES?
YES TO THE FIRST QUESTION OR THE SECOND?
EEEE... YES?
BREAK' NEWS
THANK YOU FOR TUNING IN. A LOCAL CARTOONIST HAS BEEN FOUND BEATE WITH A SUITCASE...
2016 damian

comics about
DORKBOY

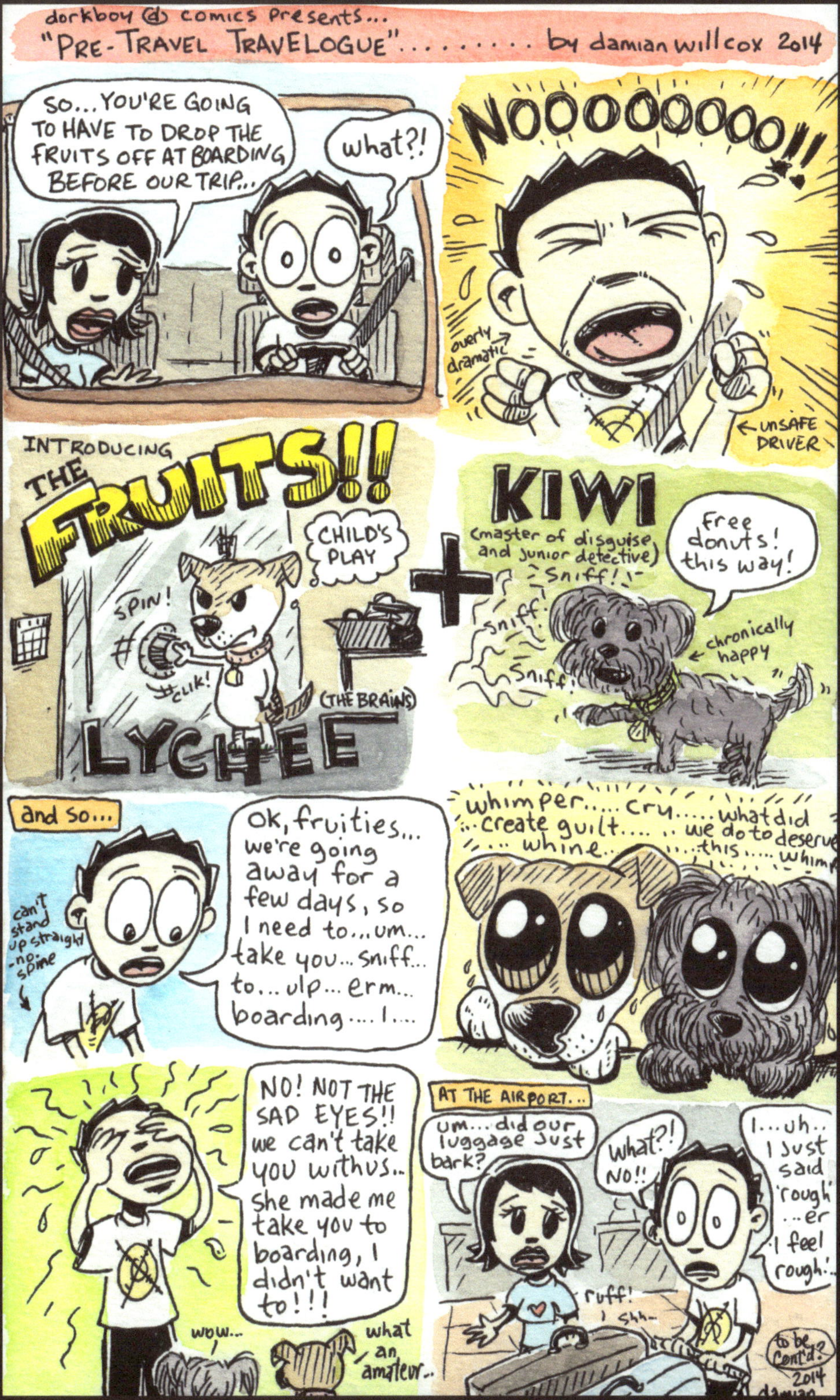
dorkboy @ comics presents...
"PRE-TRAVEL TRAVELOGUE"........ by damian willcox 2014
SO... YOU'RE GOING TO HAVE TO DROP THE FRUITS OFF AT BOARDING BEFORE OUR TRIP...
what?!
NOOOOOOOO!!
overly dramatic
UNSAFE DRIVER
INTRODUCING THE FRUITS!!
CHILD'S PLAY
SPIN!
CLIK!
(THE BRAINS)
LYCHEE
KIWI
(master of disguise and junior detective)
Free donuts! this way!
Sniff!
sniff
Sniff
chronically happy
and so...
Ok, fruities... we're going away for a few days, so I need to... um... take you... sniff... to... ulp... erm... boarding.... I...
can't stand up straight -no- spine
whimper..... cry..... create guilt..... whine.....
what did we do to deserve this..... whim
NO! NOT THE SAD EYES!! we can't take you with us.. she made me take you to boarding, I didn't want to!!!
wow...
what an amateur..
AT THE AIRPORT...
um... did our luggage just bark?
what?! NO!!
I...uh.. I just said 'rough' ...er I feel rough.'
ruff!
shh..
to be cont'd? 2014 damian

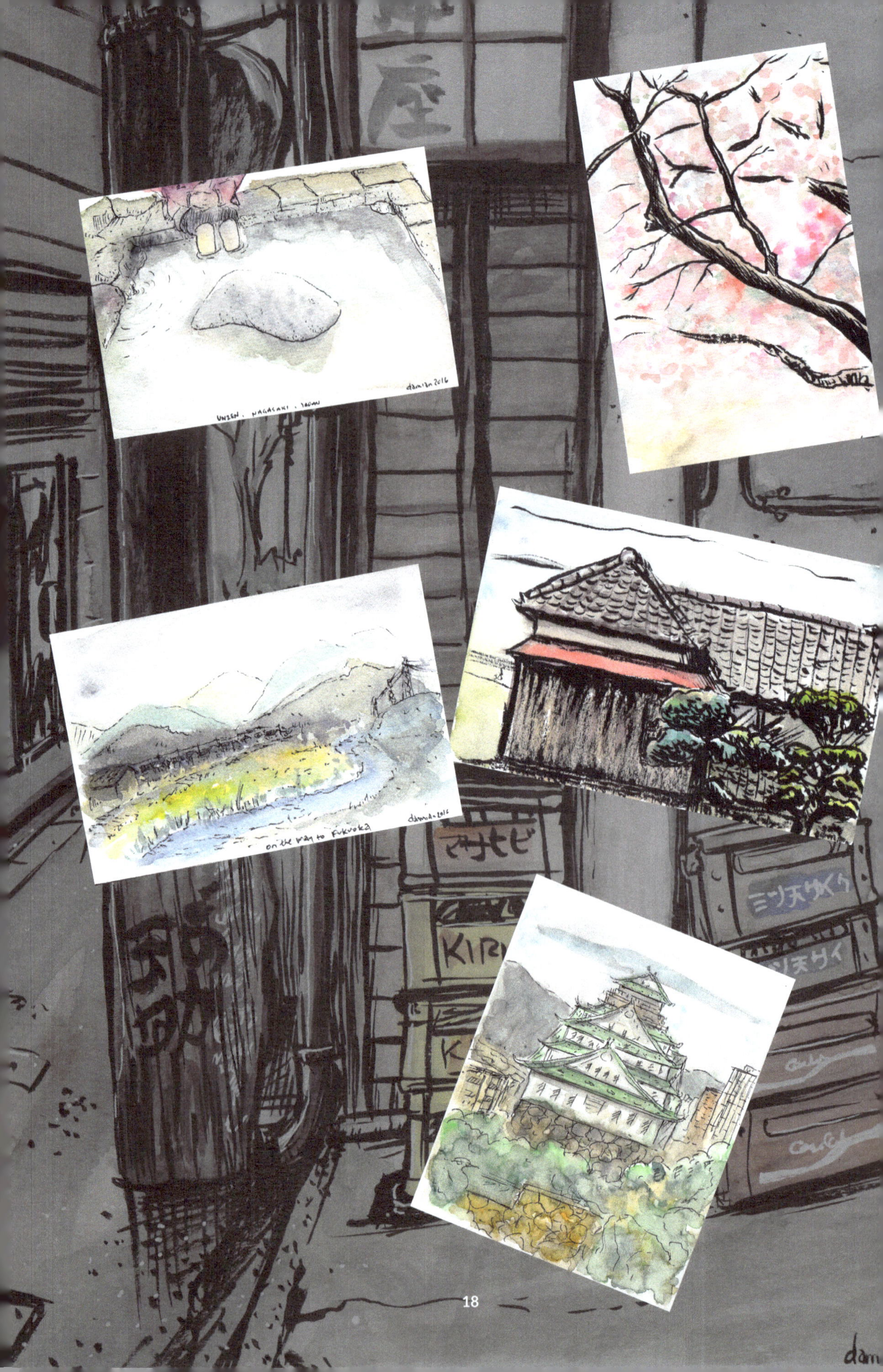

damian 2016
UNZEN . NAGASAKI . JAPAN
damian 2016
on the way to Fukuoka

comics about traveling in
JAPAN

In my travels I try to capture sketches of points of interest and of course photos, but I also like to make comics that capture the occasions, weird occurrences or even just to share bits of culture that are interesting as it serves as a better (and more entertaining) reminder than pictures or sketches alone...

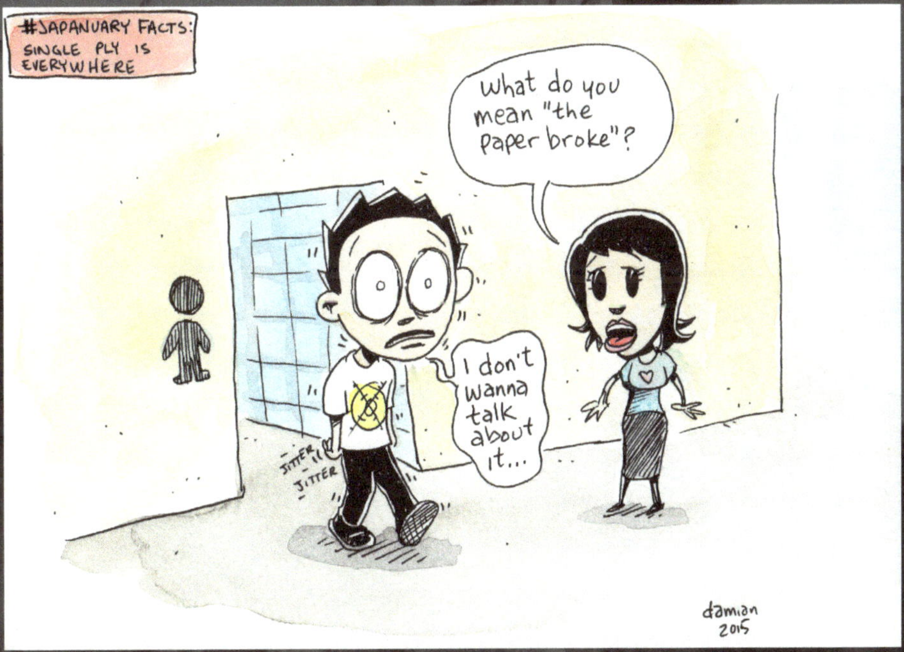
#JAPANUARY FACTS:
SINGLE PLY IS EVERYWHERE
What do you mean "the paper broke"?
I don't wanna talk about it...
JITTER JITTER
damian 2015

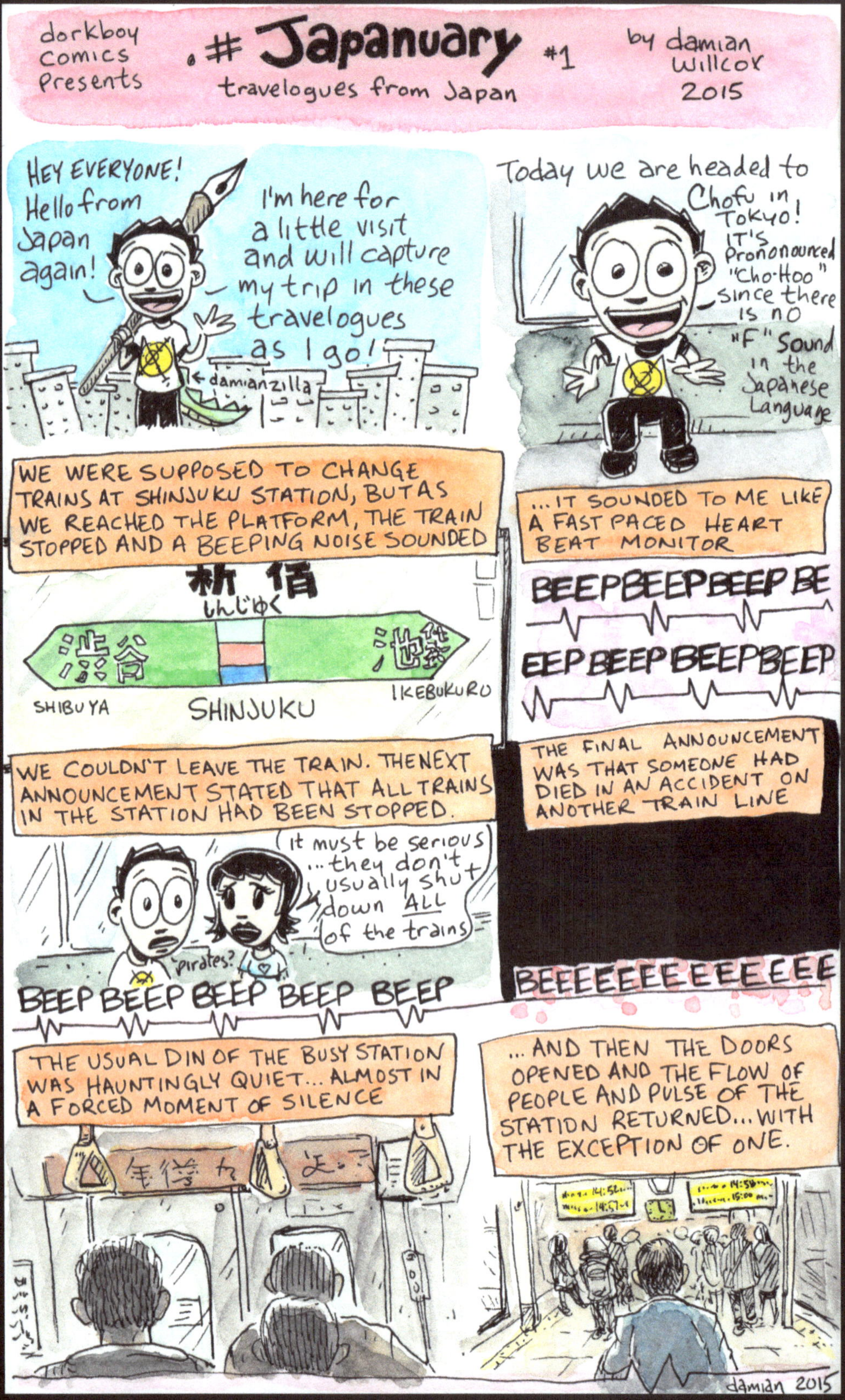
dorkboy comics presents
#Japanuary #1
travelogues from Japan
by damian willcox 2015
HEY EVERYONE! Hello from Japan again!
I'm here for a little visit and will capture my trip in these travelogues as I go!
damianzilla
Today we are headed to Chofu in Tokyo! It's pronounced "Cho-Hoo" since there is no "F" sound in the Japanese language
WE WERE SUPPOSED TO CHANGE TRAINS AT SHINJUKU STATION, BUT AS WE REACHED THE PLATFORM, THE TRAIN STOPPED AND A BEEPING NOISE SOUNDED
新宿
しんじゅく
渋谷
池袋
SHIBUYA
SHINJUKU
IKEBUKURO
...IT SOUNDED TO ME LIKE A FAST PACED HEART BEAT MONITOR
BEEPBEEPBEEPBE
EEPBEEPBEEPBEEP
WE COULDN'T LEAVE THE TRAIN. THE NEXT ANNOUNCEMENT STATED THAT ALL TRAINS IN THE STATION HAD BEEN STOPPED.
it must be serious ...they don't usually shut down ALL of the trains
pirates?
BEEP BEEP BEEP BEEP BEEP
THE FINAL ANNOUNCEMENT WAS THAT SOMEONE HAD DIED IN AN ACCIDENT ON ANOTHER TRAIN LINE
BEEEEEEEEEEEEE
THE USUAL DIN OF THE BUSY STATION WAS HAUNTINGLY QUIET... ALMOST IN A FORCED MOMENT OF SILENCE
...AND THEN THE DOORS OPENED AND THE FLOW OF PEOPLE AND PULSE OF THE STATION RETURNED... WITH THE EXCEPTION OF ONE.
damian 2015

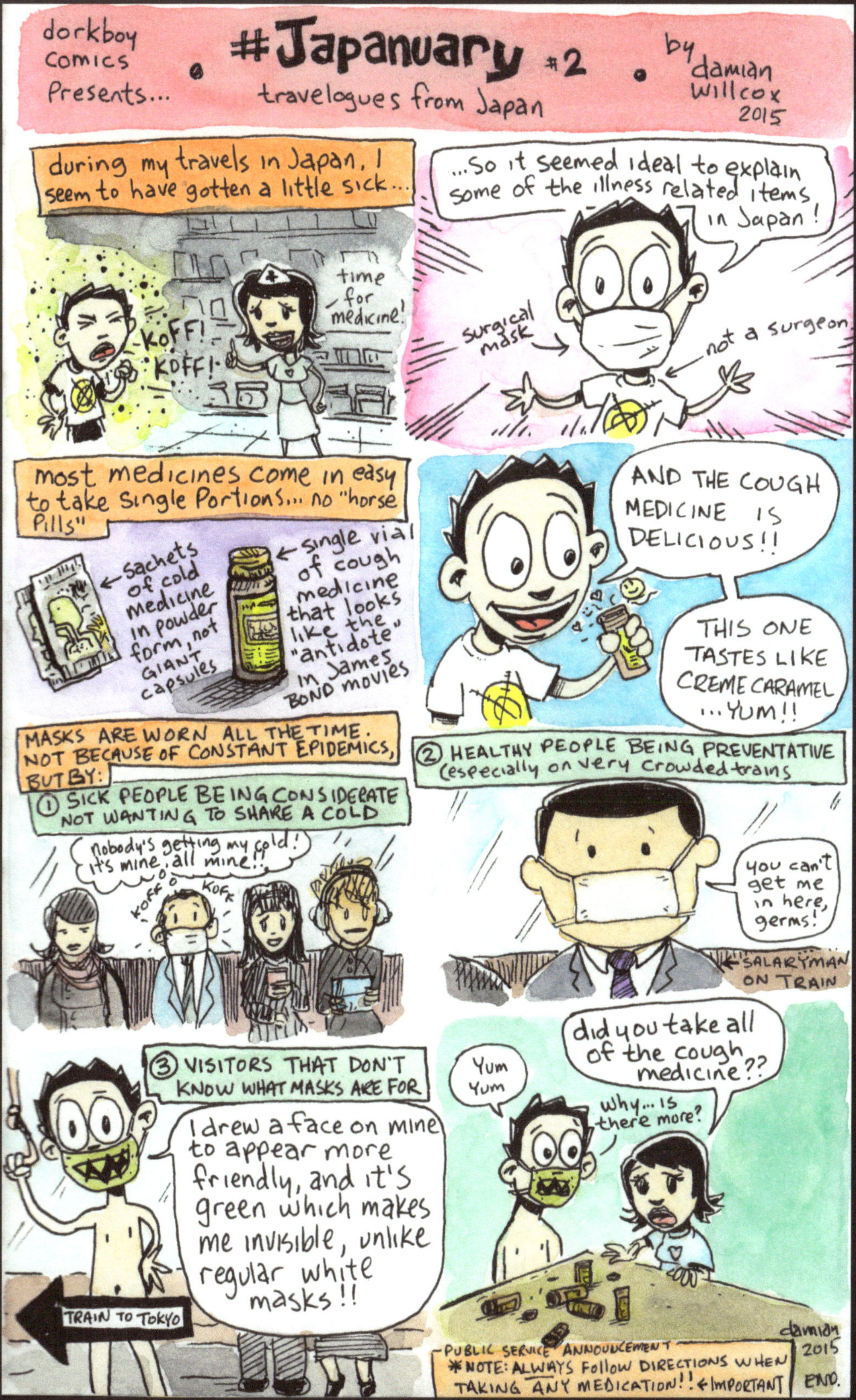

dorkboy comics Presents...
#Japanuary #2
travelogues from Japan
by damian willcox 2015
during my travels in Japan, I seem to have gotten a little sick...
KOFF! KOFF!
time for medicine!
...So it seemed ideal to explain some of the illness related items in Japan!
surgical mask
not a surgeon
most medicines come in easy to take single portions... no "horse pills"
sachets of cold medicine in powder form, not GIANT capsules
single vial of cough medicine that looks like the "antidote" in James BOND movies
AND THE COUGH MEDICINE IS DELICIOUS!!
THIS ONE TASTES LIKE CREME CARAMEL ...YUM!!
MASKS ARE WORN ALL THE TIME. NOT BECAUSE OF CONSTANT EPIDEMICS, BUT BY:
① SICK PEOPLE BEING CONSIDERATE NOT WANTING TO SHARE A COLD
Nobody's getting my cold! It's mine, all mine!!
KOFF KOFF
② HEALTHY PEOPLE BEING PREVENTATIVE (especially on very crowded trains
You can't get me in here, germs!
SALARYMAN ON TRAIN
③ VISITORS THAT DON'T KNOW WHAT MASKS ARE FOR
I drew a face on mine to appear more friendly, and it's green which makes me invisible, unlike regular white masks!!
TRAIN TO TOKYO
Yum Yum
did you take all of the cough medicine??
why... is there more?
PUBLIC SERVICE ANNOUNCEMENT
* NOTE: ALWAYS FOLLOW DIRECTIONS WHEN TAKING ANY MEDICATION!! ← IMPORTANT
damian 2015
END.

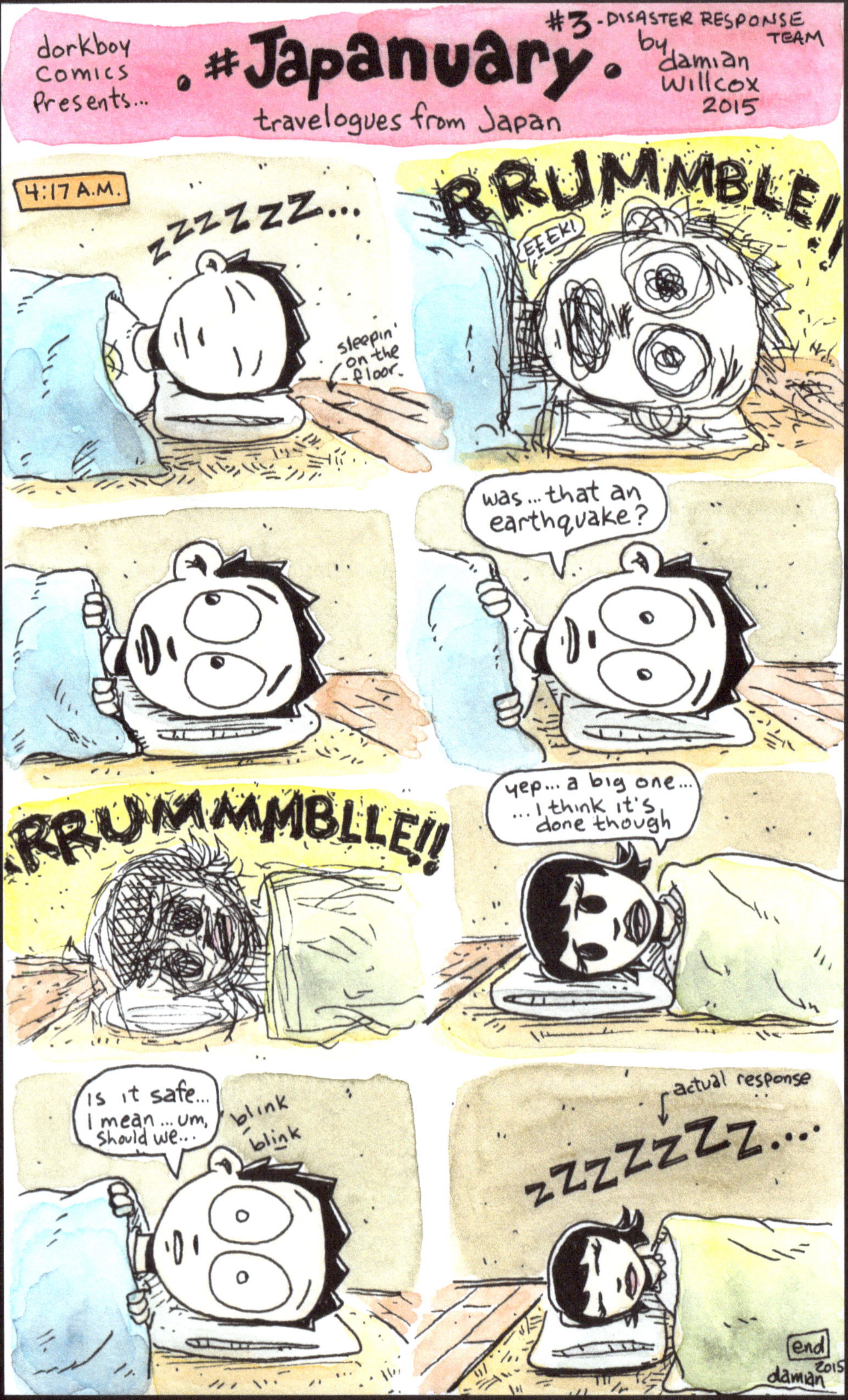
dorkboy comics presents...
#Japanuary
#3 - DISASTER RESPONSE TEAM
by damian willcox 2015
travelogues from Japan
4:17 A.M.
zzzzzz...
sleepin' on the floor.
RRUMMBLE!!
EEEK!
was... that an earthquake?
RRUMMMBLLE!!
yep... a big one...
... I think it's done though
Is it safe...
I mean... um, should we...
blink
blink
actual response
zzzzzzz...
end
damian 2015

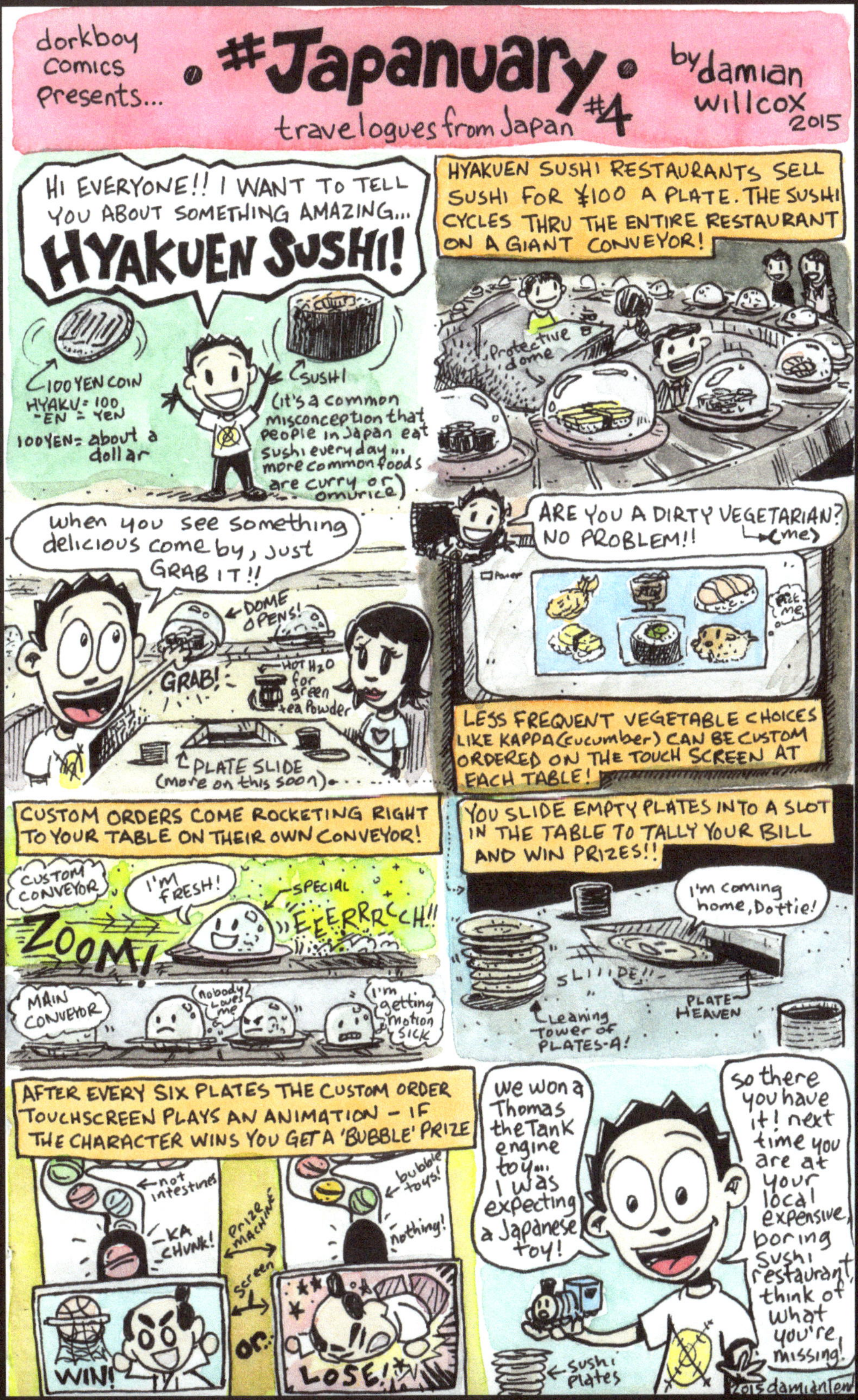

dorkboy comics presents...
#Japanuary #4
travelogues from Japan
by damian willcox 2015
HI EVERYONE!! I WANT TO TELL YOU ABOUT SOMETHING AMAZING...
HYAKUEN SUSHI!
100 YEN COIN
HYAKU = 100
-EN = YEN
100YEN = about a dollar
SUSHI
(it's a common misconception that people in Japan eat sushi every day... more common foods are curry or omurice)
HYAKUEN SUSHI RESTAURANTS SELL SUSHI FOR ¥100 A PLATE. THE SUSHI CYCLES THRU THE ENTIRE RESTAURANT ON A GIANT CONVEYOR!
protective dome
when you see something delicious come by, just GRAB IT!!
DOME OPENS!
GRAB!
HOT H2O for green tea powder
PLATE SLIDE (more on this soon)
ARE YOU A DIRTY VEGETARIAN? NO PROBLEM!!
me
Pick me
LESS FREQUENT VEGETABLE CHOICES LIKE KAPPA (cucumber) CAN BE CUSTOM ORDERED ON THE TOUCH SCREEN AT EACH TABLE!
CUSTOM ORDERS COME ROCKETING RIGHT TO YOUR TABLE ON THEIR OWN CONVEYOR!
CUSTOM CONVEYOR
I'M FRESH!
SPECIAL
EEERRRCCH!!
ZOOM!
MAIN CONVEYOR
nobody loves me
I'm getting motion sick
YOU SLIDE EMPTY PLATES INTO A SLOT IN THE TABLE TO TALLY YOUR BILL AND WIN PRIZES!!
I'm coming home, Dottie!
SLIIIDE!!
Leaning Tower of PLATES-A!
PLATE HEAVEN
AFTER EVERY SIX PLATES THE CUSTOM ORDER TOUCHSCREEN PLAYS AN ANIMATION - IF THE CHARACTER WINS YOU GET A 'BUBBLE' PRIZE
not intestines
KA CHUNK!
prize machine
bubble toys!
nothing!
screen
or
WIN!
LOSE!
we won a Thomas the Tank engine toy... I was expecting a Japanese toy!
so there you have it! next time you are at your local expensive boring sushi restaurant, think of what you're missing!
sushi plates
2015 damian tew

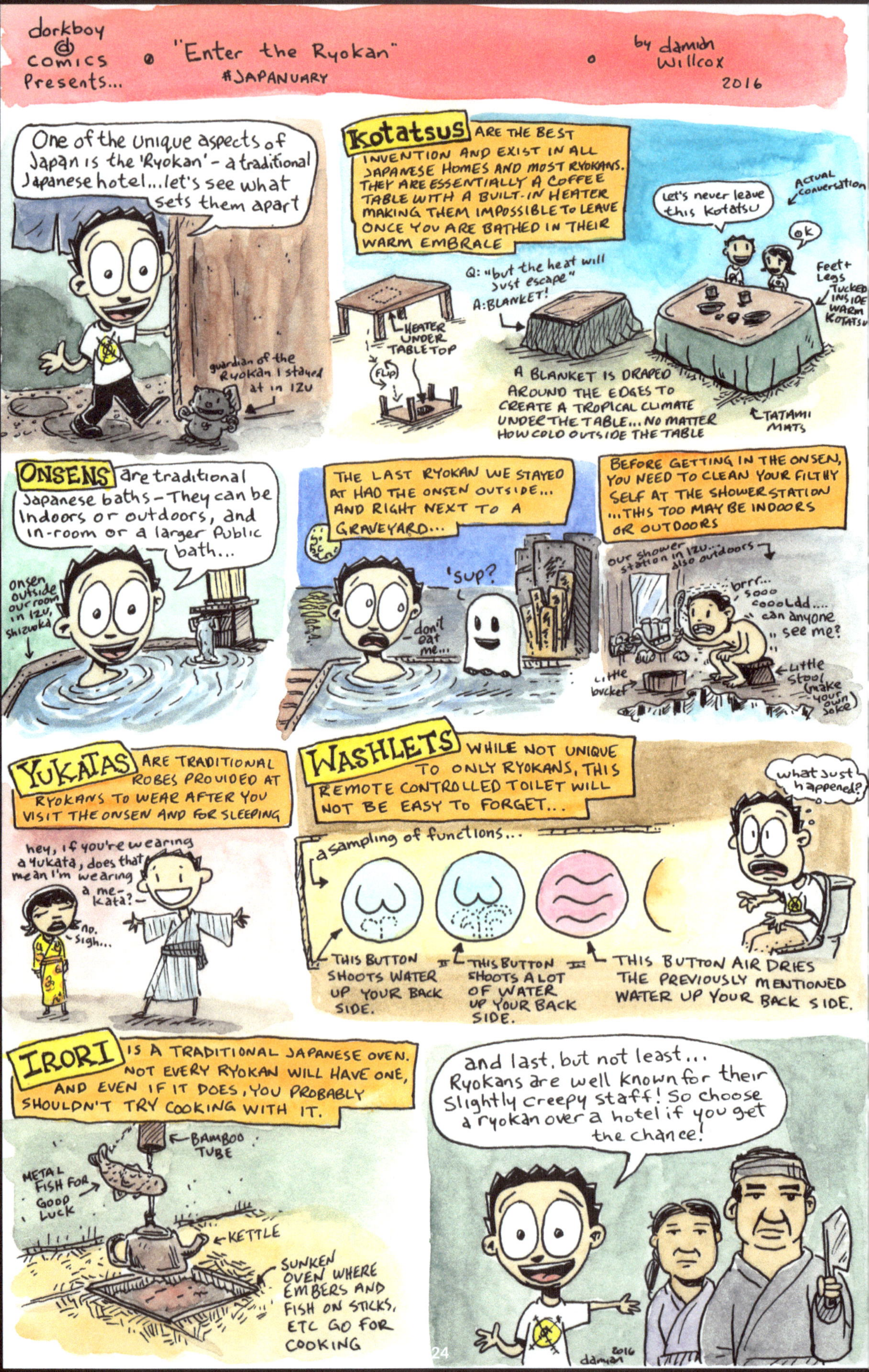
dorkboy comics Presents...
"Enter the Ryokan"
#JAPANUARY
by damian Willcox 2016
One of the unique aspects of Japan is the 'Ryokan' - a traditional Japanese hotel... let's see what sets them apart
guardian of the Ryokan I stayed at in IZU
Kotatsus are the best invention and exist in all Japanese homes and most Ryokans. They are essentially a coffee table with a built-in heater making them impossible to leave once you are bathed in their warm embrace
Let's never leave this kotatsu
ok
Actual conversation
Q: "but the heat will just escape"
A: BLANKET!
Heater under tabletop
Flip
Feet + Legs tucked inside warm kotatsu
A blanket is draped around the edges to create a tropical climate under the table... no matter how cold outside the table
Tatami mats
ONSENS are traditional Japanese baths - They can be Indoors or outdoors, and in-room or a larger public bath...
onsen outside our room in Izu, Shizuoka
The last ryokan we stayed at had the onsen outside... and right next to a graveyard...
'sup?
don't eat me...
Before getting in the onsen, you need to clean your filthy self at the shower station ... this too may be indoors or outdoors
our shower station in Izu... also outdoors
brrr... sooo coooldd.... can anyone see me?
Little bucket
Little stool (make your own joke)
YUKATAS are traditional robes provided at ryokans to wear after you visit the onsen and for sleeping
hey, if you're wearing a yukata, does that mean I'm wearing a me-kata?
no. sigh...
WASHLETS while not unique to only ryokans, this remote controlled toilet will not be easy to forget...
a sampling of functions...
what just happened?
This button shoots water up your back side.
II This button shoots a lot of water up your back side.
III This button air dries the previously mentioned water up your back side.
IRORI is a traditional Japanese oven. Not every ryokan will have one, and even if it does, you probably shouldn't try cooking with it.
Bamboo tube
Metal fish for good luck
Kettle
Sunken oven where embers and fish on sticks, etc go for cooking
and last, but not least... Ryokans are well known for their slightly creepy staff! So choose a ryokan over a hotel if you get the chance!
damian 2016

comics about traveling in NORTH AMERICA

Road trips are adventures all their own, and sometimes you just need to capture driving through a deserted part of Vancouver Island at 2 a.m. en route to your destination to remind yourself to not do it again.

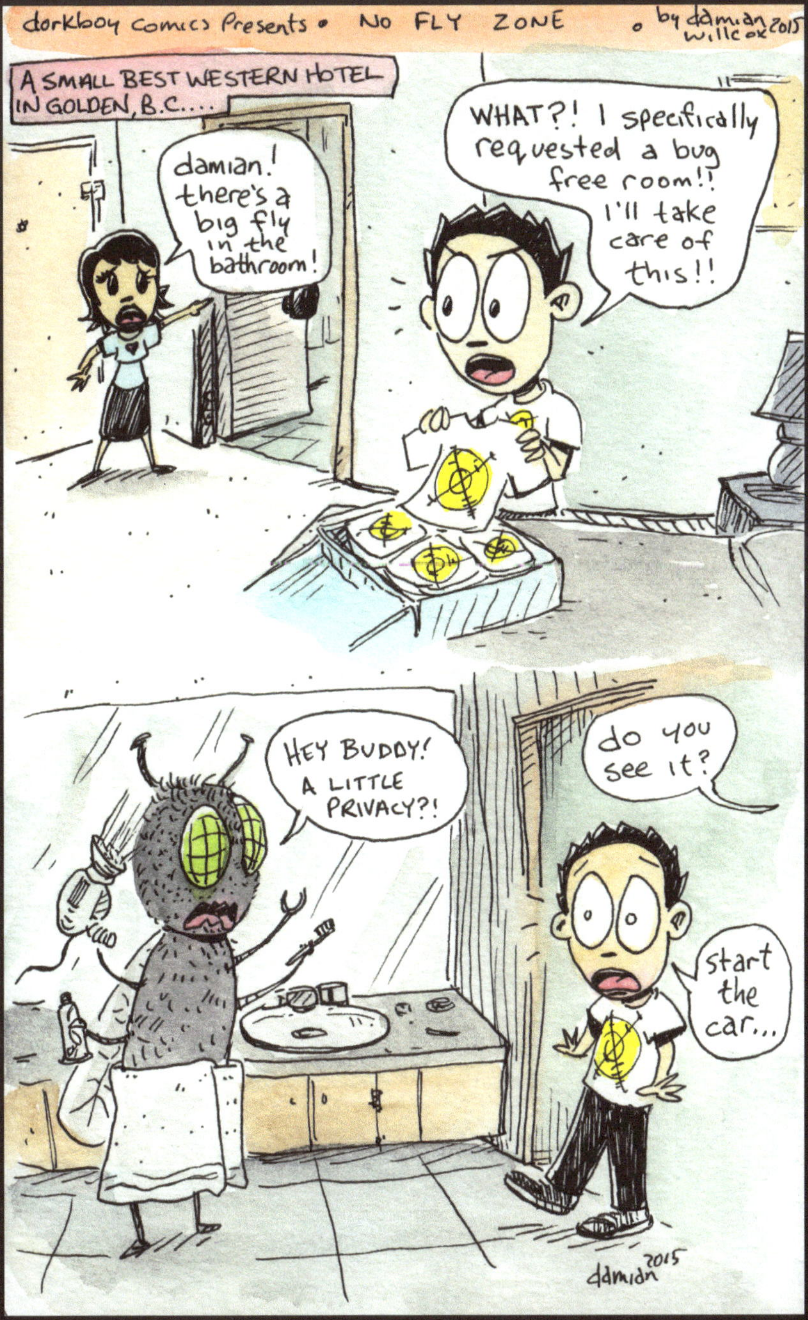
dorkboy comics presents • NO FLY ZONE • by damian willcox 2015
A SMALL BEST WESTERN HOTEL IN GOLDEN, B.C....
damian! there's a big fly in the bathroom!
WHAT?! I specifically requested a bug free room!! I'll take care of this!!
HEY BUDDY! A LITTLE PRIVACY?!
do you see it?
start the car...
damian 2015

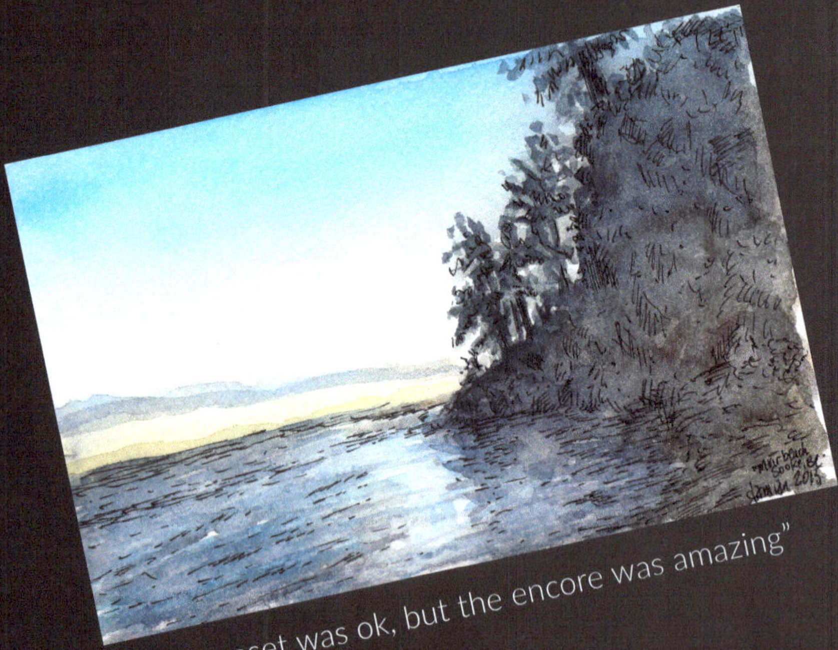
Sooke BC
damian 2015

"The sunset was ok, but the encore was amazing"

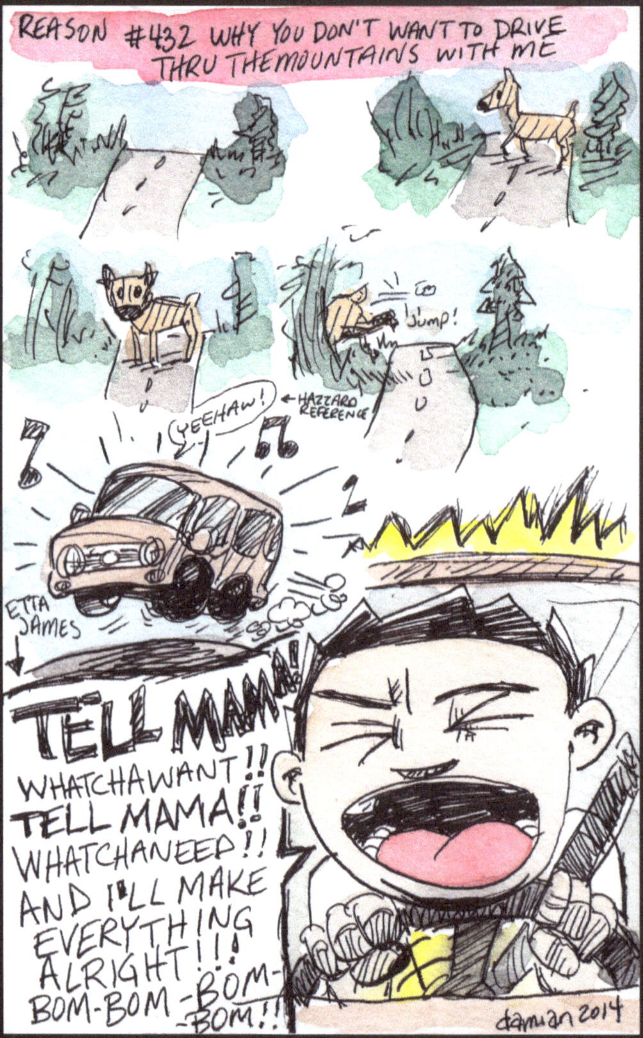
REASON #432 WHY YOU DON'T WANT TO DRIVE THRU THEMOUNTAINS WITH ME
JUMP!
YEEHAW!
← HAZZARD REFERENCE
ETTA JAMES
TELL MAMA!
WHATCHAWANT!!
TELL MAMA!!
WHATCHANEED!!
AND I'LL MAKE
EVERYTHING
ALRIGHT!!!
BOM-BOM-BOM-BOM!!
damian 2014

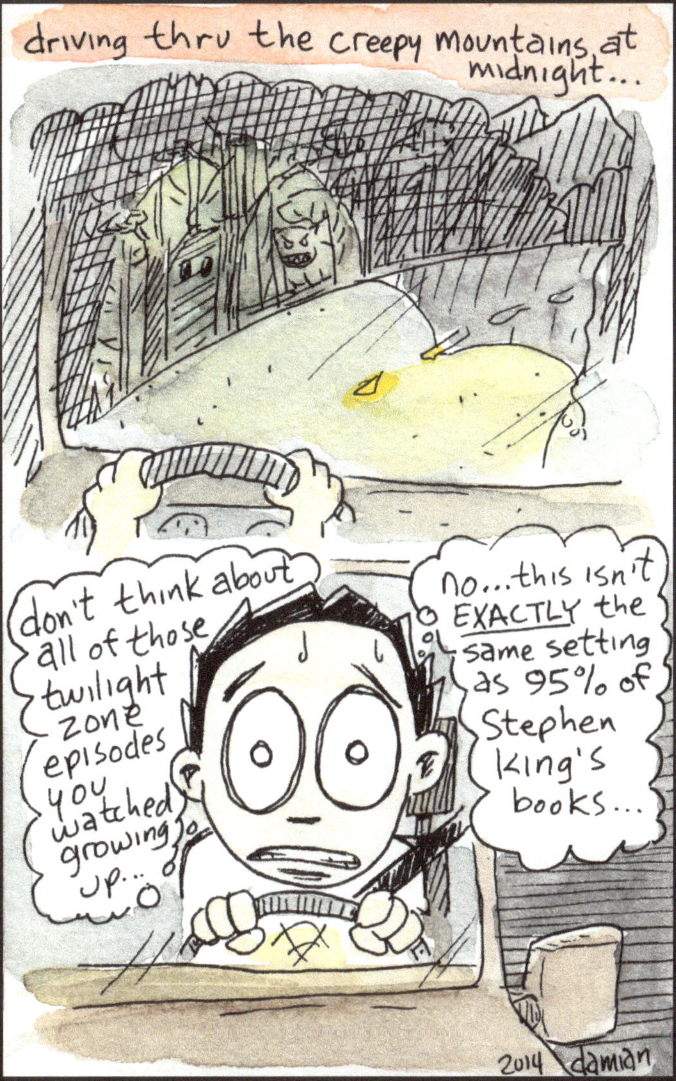
driving thru the creepy mountains at midnight...
don't think about all of those twilight zone episodes you watched growing up...
no...this isn't EXACTLY the same setting as 95% of Stephen King's books...
2014 damian

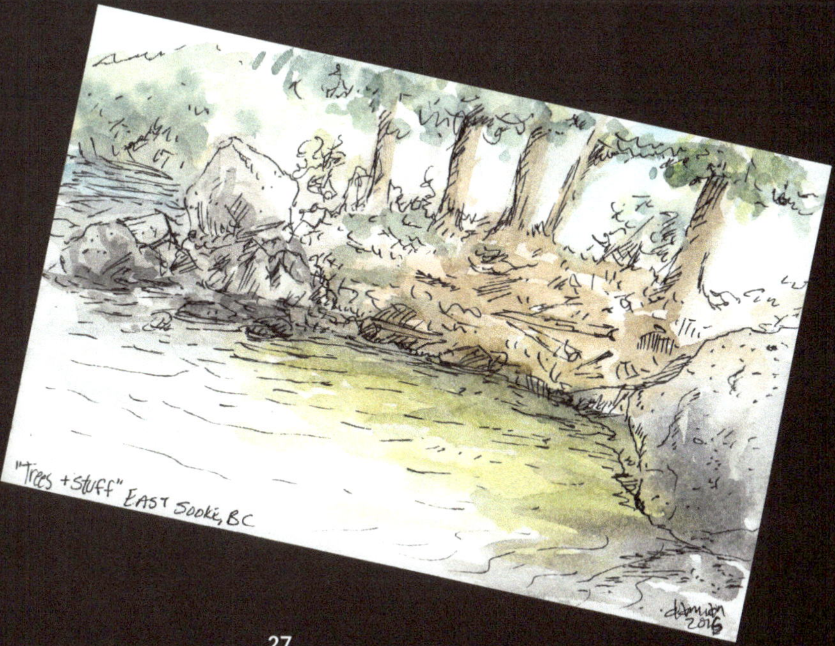
"Trees + Stuff" EAST SOOKE, BC
damian 2016

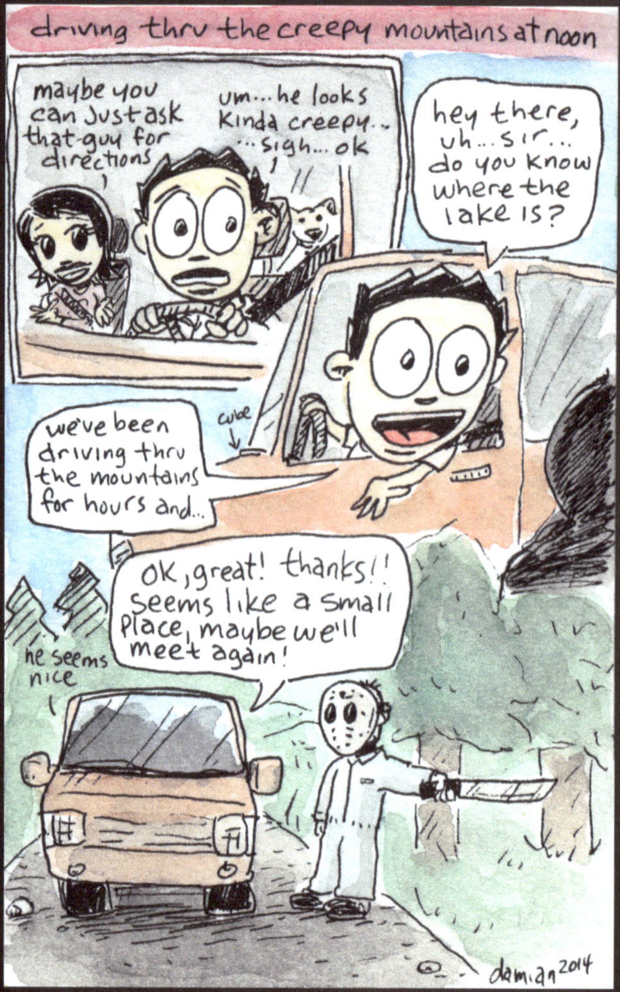
driving thru the creepy mountains at noon
maybe you can just ask that guy for directions
um... he looks kinda creepy... ...sigh... ok
hey there, uh... sir... do you know where the lake is?
cube
we've been driving thru the mountains for hours and...
OK, great! thanks!! seems like a small place, maybe we'll meet again!
he seems nice
damian 2014

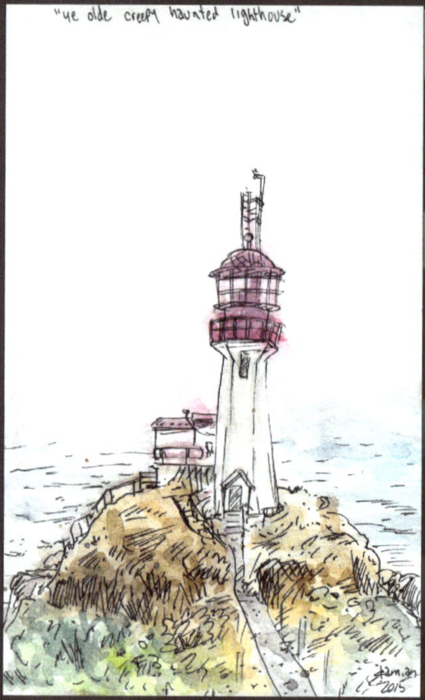
"ye olde creepy haunted lighthouse"
damian 2015

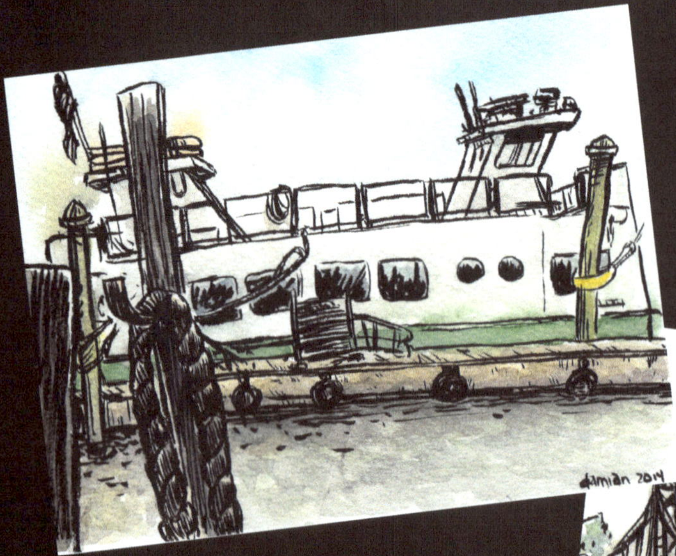
damian 2014

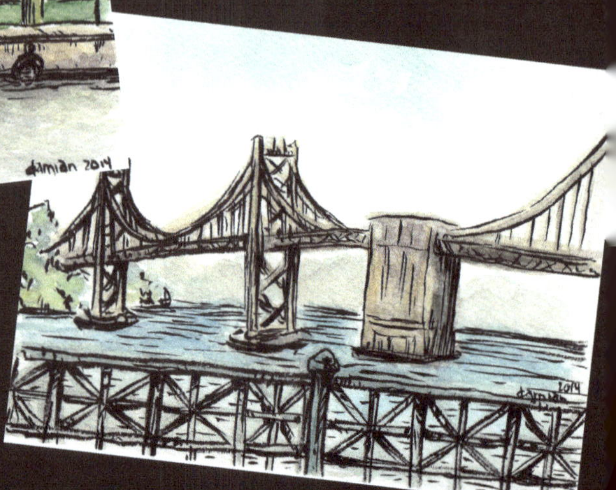

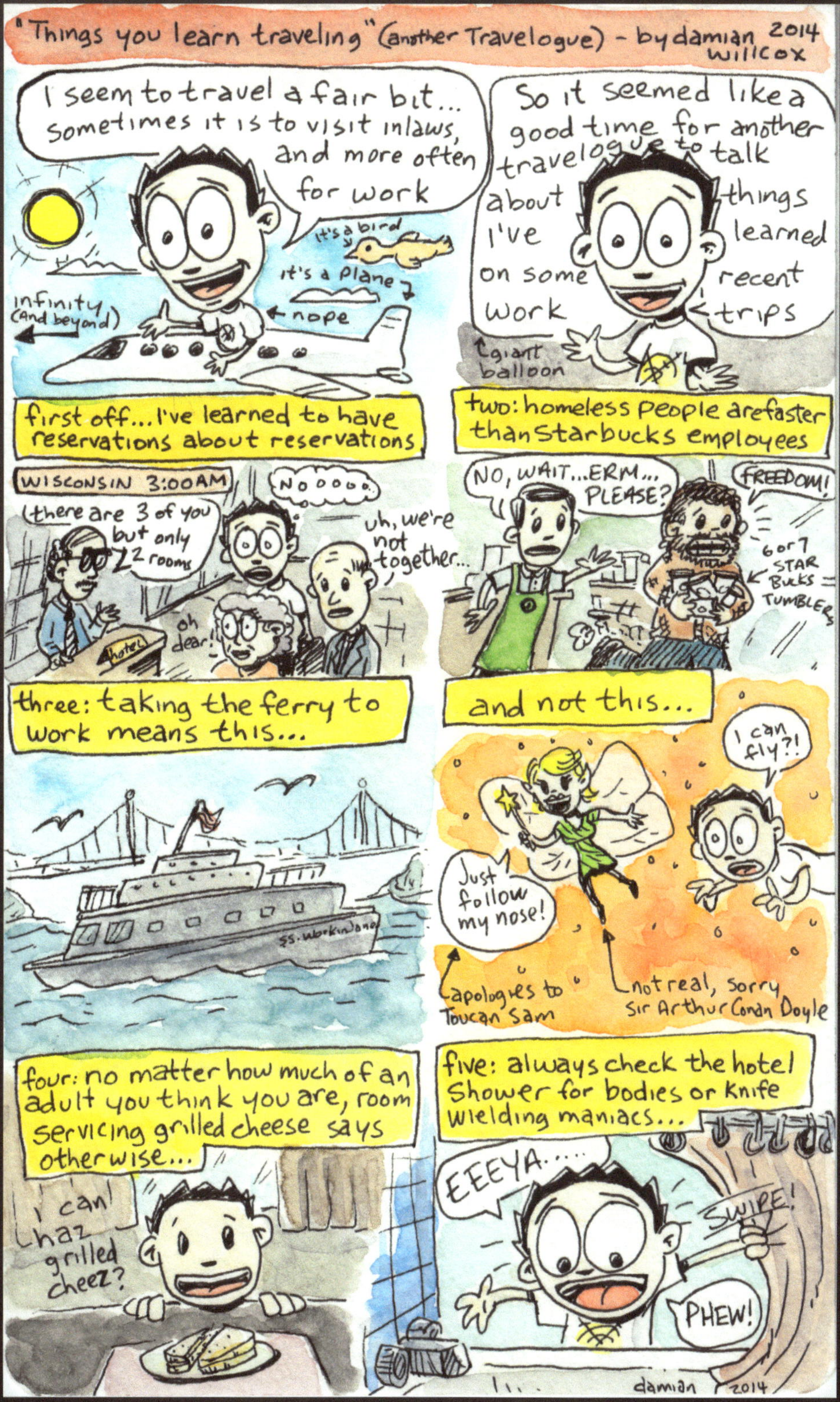
"Things you learn traveling" (another Travelogue) - by damian willcox 2014
I seem to travel a fair bit... sometimes it is to visit inlaws, and more often for work
it's a bird
it's a plane
nope
infinity (and beyond)
So it seemed like a good time for another travelogue to talk about things I've learned on some recent work trips
giant balloon
first off... I've learned to have reservations about reservations
WISCONSIN 3:00AM
there are 3 of you but only 2 rooms
Noooo
uh, we're not together...
oh dear!
hotel
two: homeless people are faster than Starbucks employees
NO, WAIT...ERM... PLEASE?
FREEDOM!
6 or 7 STAR BUCKS TUMBLERS
three: taking the ferry to work means this...
S.S. workinland
and not this...
I can fly?!
Just follow my nose!
apologies to Toucan Sam
not real, sorry Sir Arthur Conan Doyle
four: no matter how much of an adult you think you are, room servicing grilled cheese says otherwise...
I can haz grilled cheez?
five: always check the hotel shower for bodies or knife wielding maniacs...
EEEYA....
SWIPE!
PHEW!
damian 2014

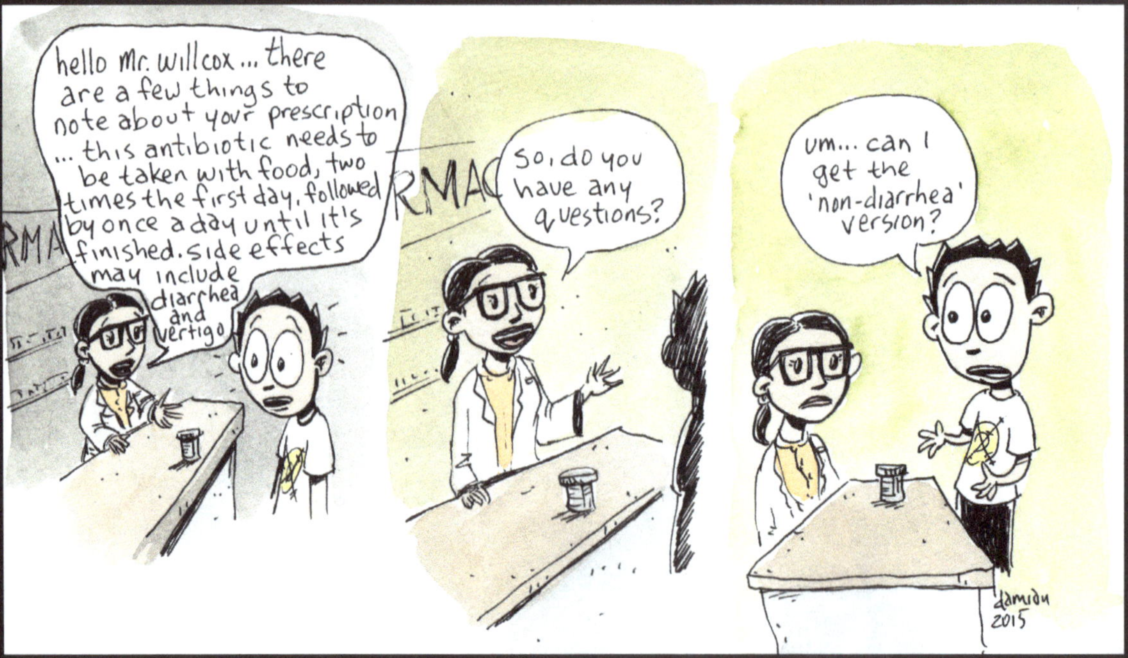
hello mr. willcox ... there are a few things to note about your prescription ... this antibiotic needs to be taken with food, two times the first day, followed by once a day until it's finished. side effects may include diarrhea and vertigo
so, do you have any questions?
um... can I get the 'non-diarrhea' version?
damian 2015

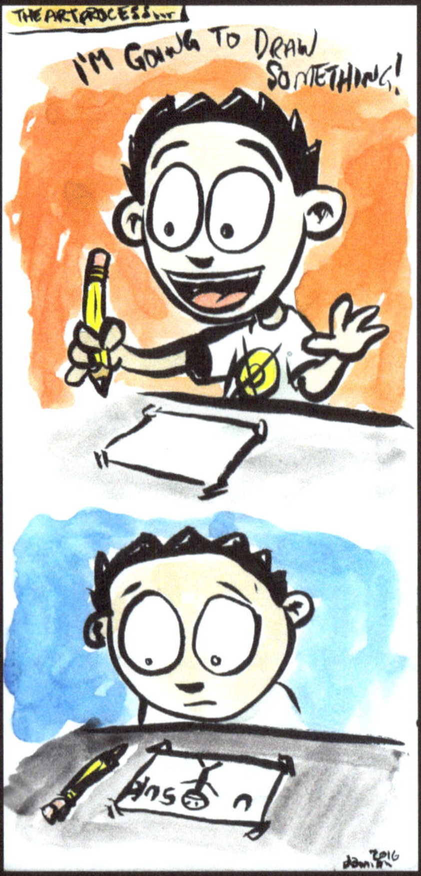
THE ART PROCESS...
I'M GOING TO DRAW SOMETHING!

comics about
LIFE

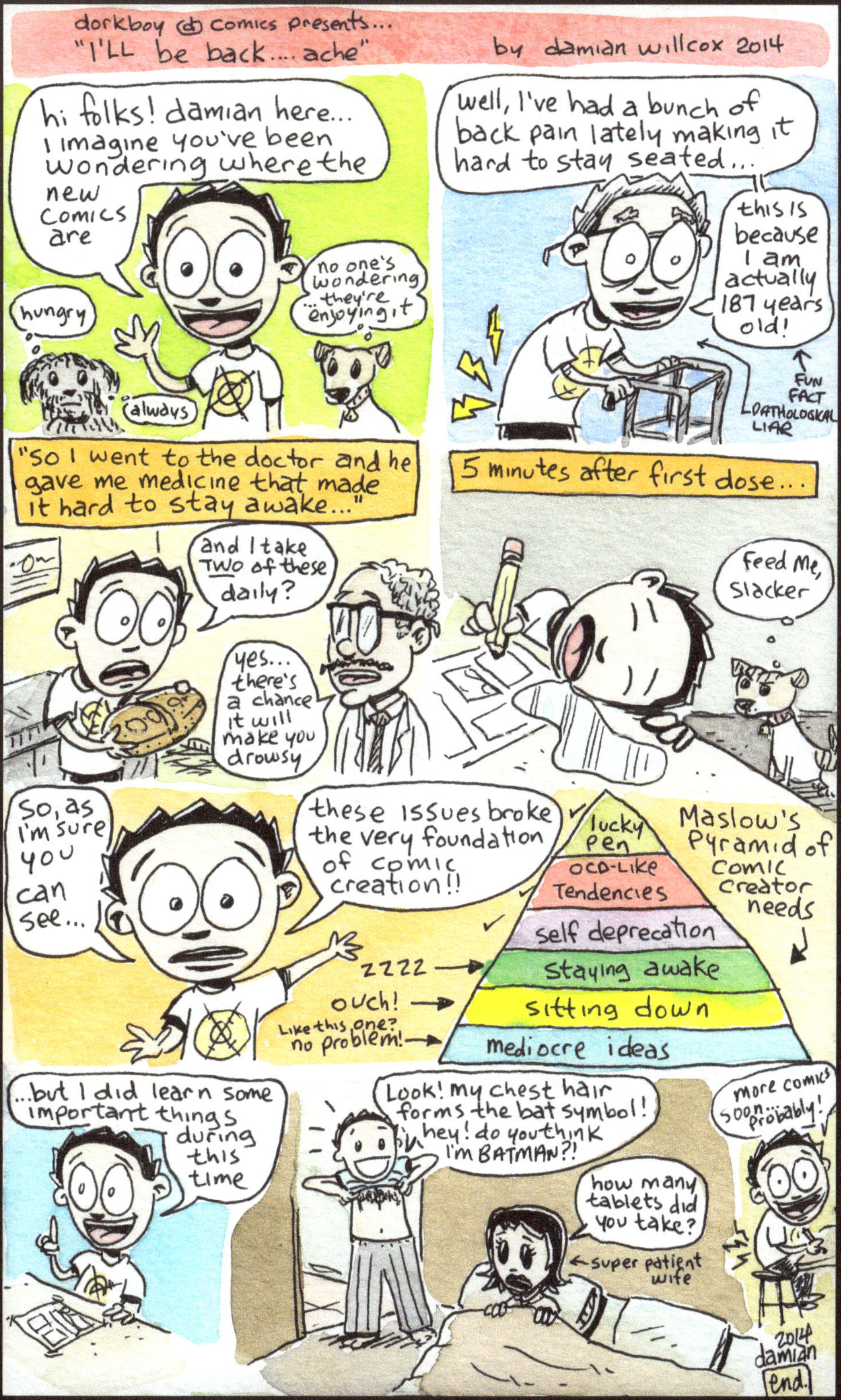

dorkboy comics presents...
"I'LL be back.... ache"
by damian willcox 2014
hi folks! damian here... I imagine you've been wondering where the new comics are
hungry
always
no one's wondering ...they're enjoying it
well, I've had a bunch of back pain lately making it hard to stay seated...
this is because I am actually 187 years old!
FUN FACT
PATHOLOGICAL LIAR
"so I went to the doctor and he gave me medicine that made it hard to stay awake..."
and I take TWO of these daily?
yes... there's a chance it will make you drowsy
5 minutes after first dose...
Feed Me, Slacker
So, as I'm sure you can see...
these issues broke the very foundation of comic creation!!
Maslow's Pyramid of Comic Creator needs
lucky pen
OCD-Like Tendencies
self deprecation
staying awake
sitting down
mediocre ideas
zzzz
ouch!
Like this one? no problem!
...but I did learn some important things during this time
Look! my chest hair forms the bat symbol! hey! do you think I'm BATMAN?!
how many tablets did you take?
super patient wife
more comics soon... probably!
2014 damian
end.

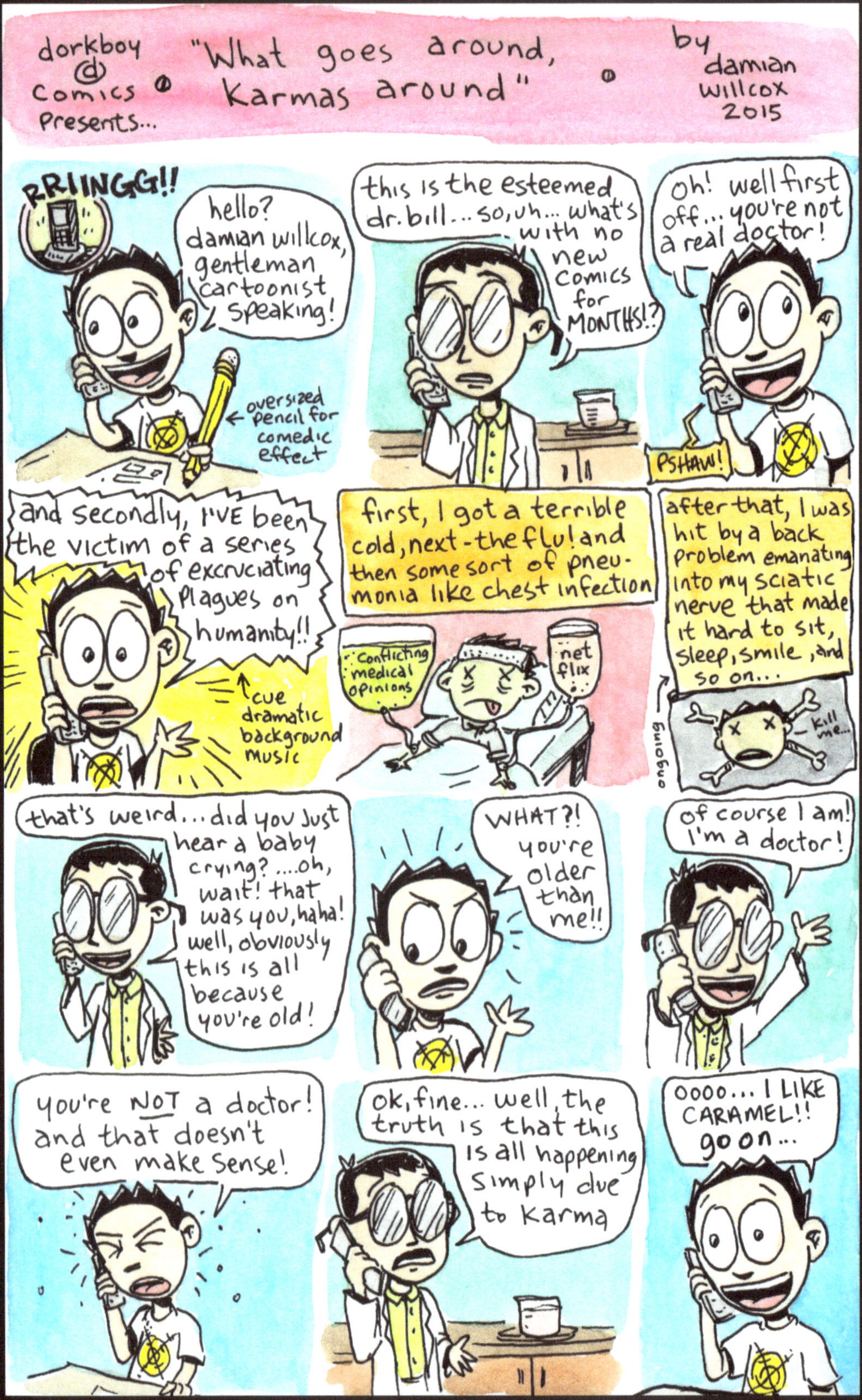

dorkboy comics presents...
"What goes around, Karmas around"
by damian willcox 2015
RRIINGG!!
hello? damian willcox, gentleman cartoonist speaking!
oversized pencil for comedic effect
this is the esteemed dr. bill... so, uh... what's with no new comics for MONTHS!?
oh! well first off... you're not a real doctor!
PSHAW!
and secondly, I'VE been the victim of a series of excruciating plagues on humanity!!
cue dramatic background music
first, I got a terrible cold, next - the flu! and then some sort of pneu-monia like chest infection
conflicting medical opinions
net flix
after that, I was hit by a back problem emanating into my sciatic nerve that made it hard to sit, sleep, smile, and so on...
ongoing
kill me...
that's weird... did you just hear a baby crying? ....oh, wait! that was you, haha! well, obviously this is all because you're old!
WHAT?! you're older than me!!
of course I am! I'm a doctor!
you're NOT a doctor! and that doesn't even make sense!
ok, fine... well, the truth is that this is all happening simply due to karma
OOOO... I LIKE CARAMEL!! go on...

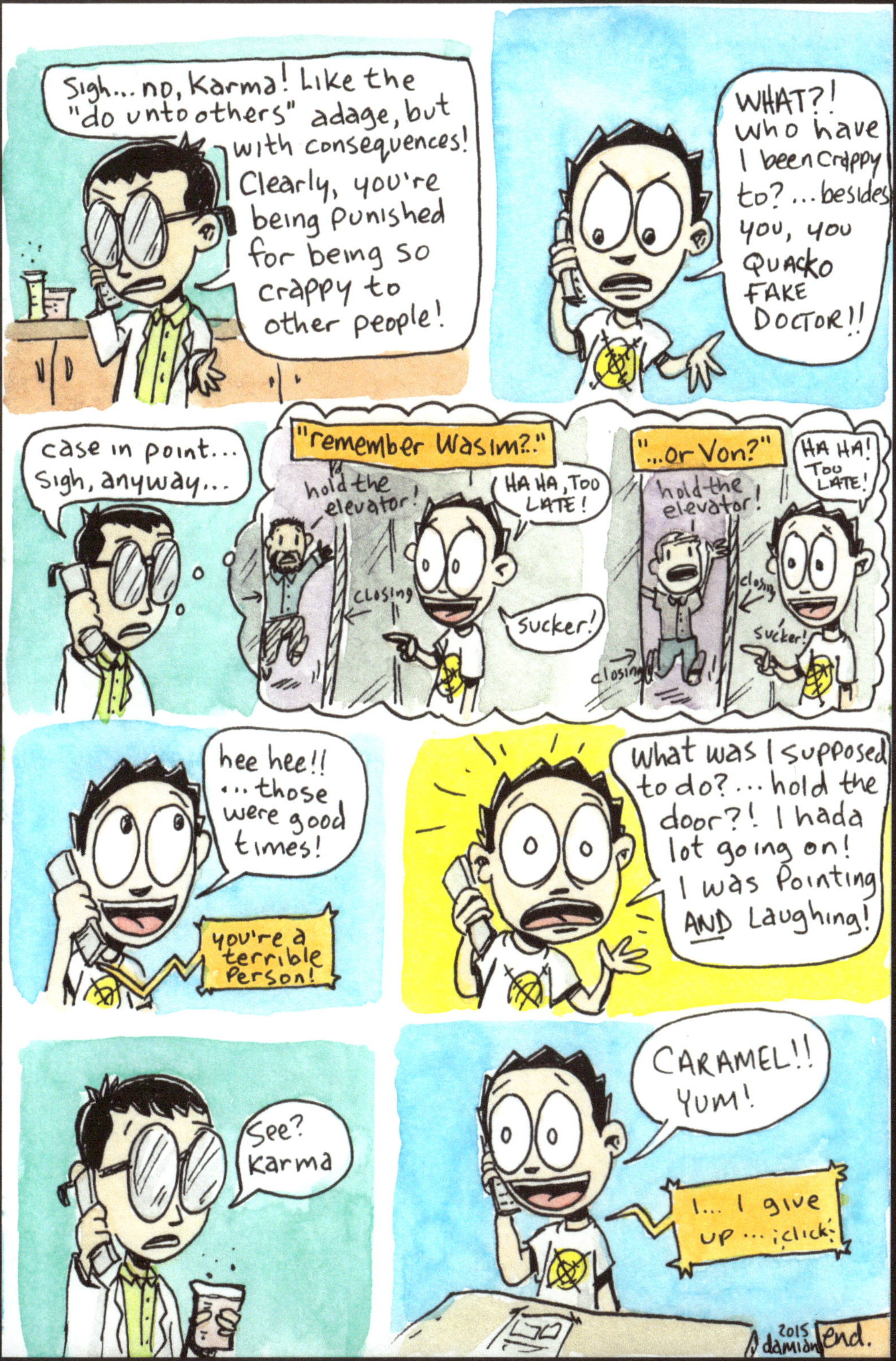

Sigh... no, Karma! Like the "do unto others" adage, but with consequences! Clearly, you're being punished for being so crappy to other people!
WHAT?! who have I been crappy to? ...besides you, you QUACKO FAKE DOCTOR!!
case in point... Sigh, anyway...
"remember Wasim?."
hold the elevator!
HA HA, TOO LATE!
closing
sucker!
"...or Von?"
hold the elevator!
HA HA! TOO LATE!
closing
sucker!
closing
hee hee!! ...those were good times!
you're a terrible person!
what was I supposed to do? ...hold the door?! I hada lot going on! I was Pointing AND Laughing!
See? Karma
CARAMEL!! YUM!
I... I give up ... ¡click!
2015 damian
end.

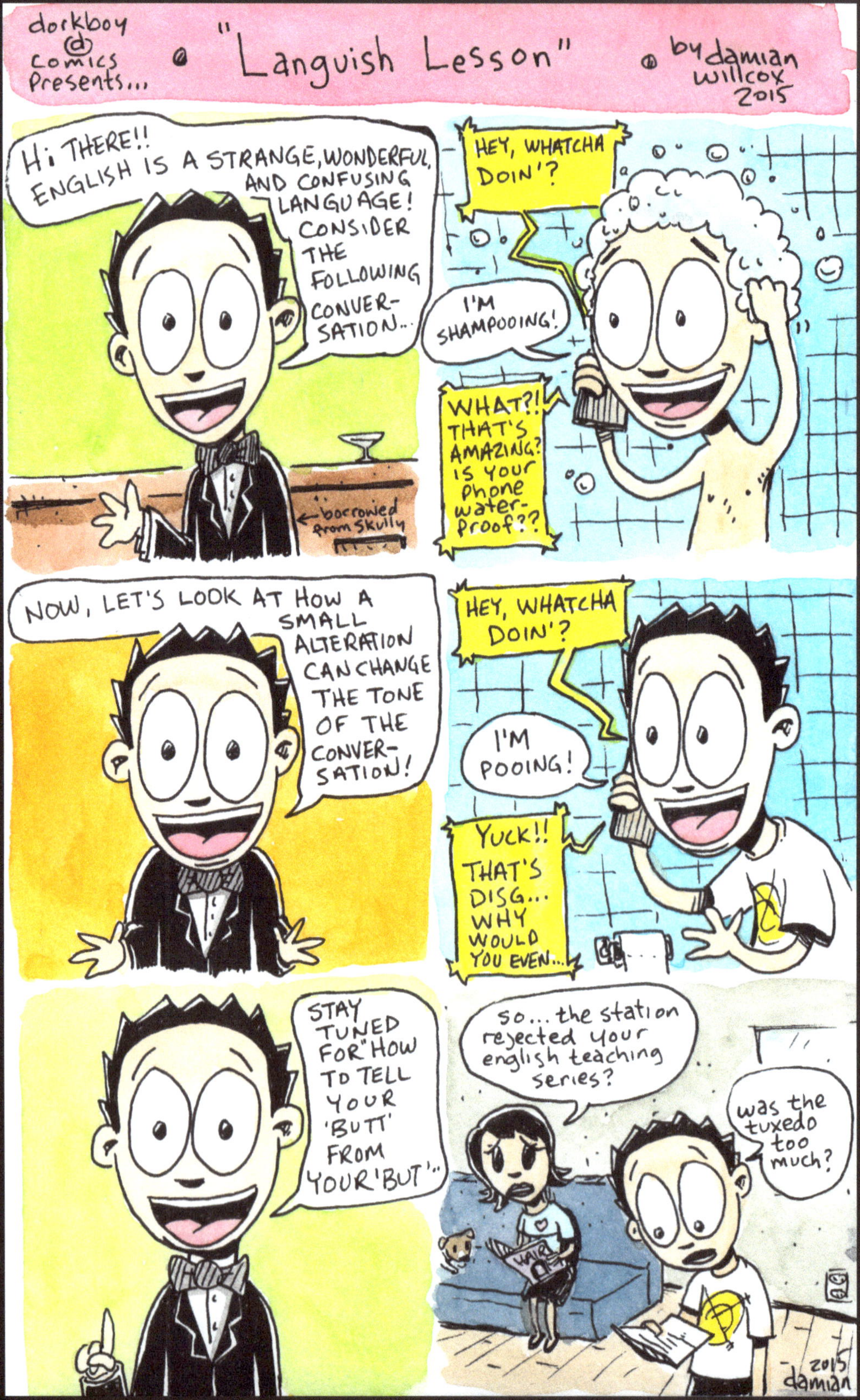
dorkboy comics presents...
"Languish Lesson"
by damian willcox 2015
Hi THERE!! ENGLISH IS A STRANGE, WONDERFUL, AND CONFUSING LANGUAGE! CONSIDER THE FOLLOWING CONVERSATION...
borrowed from skully
HEY, WHATCHA DOIN'?
I'M SHAMPOOING!
WHAT?!! THAT'S AMAZING? IS YOUR PHONE WATERPROOF??
NOW, LET'S LOOK AT HOW A SMALL ALTERATION CAN CHANGE THE TONE OF THE CONVERSATION!
HEY, WHATCHA DOIN'?
I'M POOING!
YUCK!! THAT'S DISG... WHY WOULD YOU EVEN...
STAY TUNED FOR "HOW TO TELL YOUR 'BUTT' FROM YOUR 'BUT'"..
so... the station rejected your english teaching series?
was the tuxedo too much?
2015 damian

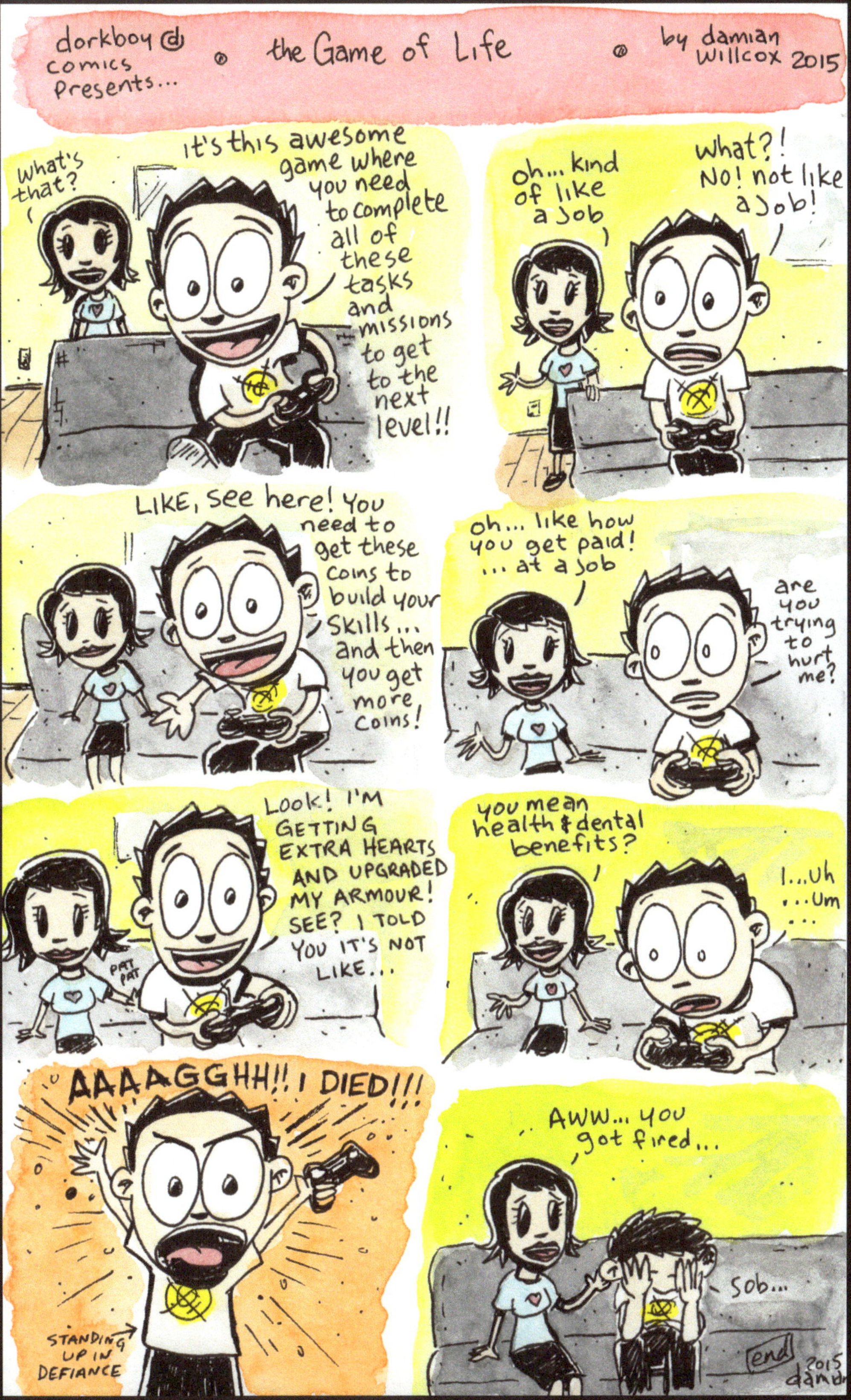
dorkboy comics presents...
the Game of Life
by damian willcox 2015
what's that?
it's this awesome game where you need to complete all of these tasks and missions to get to the next level!!
oh... kind of like a job
what?! No! not like a job!
LIKE, see here! You need to get these coins to build your skills... and then you get more coins!
oh... like how you get paid! ... at a job
are you trying to hurt me?
Look! I'M GETTING EXTRA HEARTS AND UPGRADED MY ARMOUR! SEE? I TOLD YOU IT'S NOT LIKE...
PAT PAT
you mean health & dental benefits?
I...uh ...Um ...
AAAAGGHH!! I DIED!!!
STANDING UP IN DEFIANCE
AWW... you got fired...
sob...
end
2015 dam

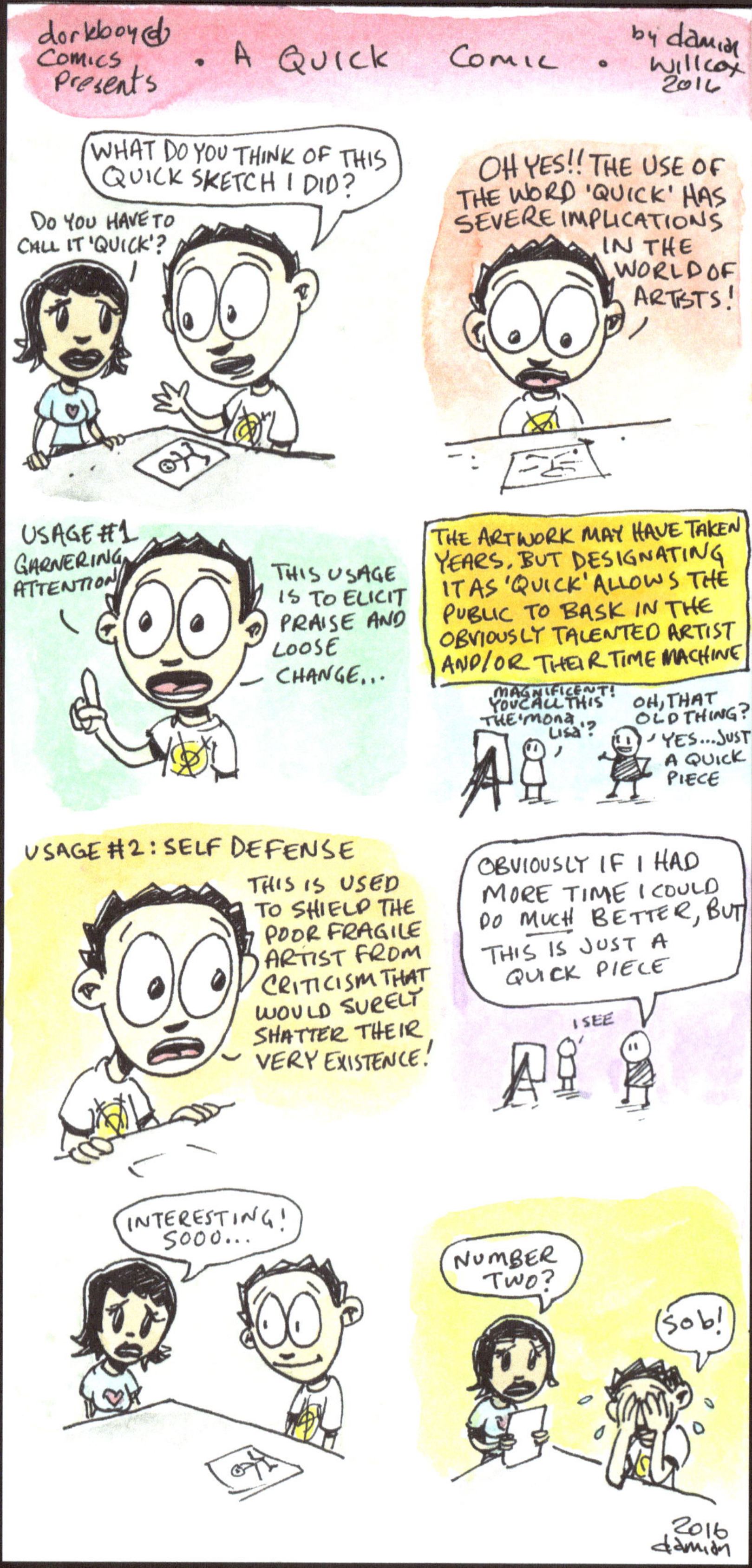
dorkboy comics presents • A Quick Comic • by damian willcox 2016
WHAT DO YOU THINK OF THIS QUICK SKETCH I DID?
DO YOU HAVE TO CALL IT 'QUICK'?
OH YES!! THE USE OF THE WORD 'QUICK' HAS SEVERE IMPLICATIONS IN THE WORLD OF ARTISTS!
USAGE #1 GARNERING ATTENTION
THIS USAGE IS TO ELICIT PRAISE AND LOOSE CHANGE...
THE ARTWORK MAY HAVE TAKEN YEARS, BUT DESIGNATING IT AS 'QUICK' ALLOWS THE PUBLIC TO BASK IN THE OBVIOUSLY TALENTED ARTIST AND/OR THEIR TIME MACHINE
MAGNIFICENT! YOU CALL THIS THE 'mona Lisa'?
OH, THAT OLD THING? YES...JUST A QUICK PIECE
USAGE #2: SELF DEFENSE
THIS IS USED TO SHIELD THE POOR FRAGILE ARTIST FROM CRITICISM THAT WOULD SURELY SHATTER THEIR VERY EXISTENCE!
OBVIOUSLY IF I HAD MORE TIME I COULD DO MUCH BETTER, BUT THIS IS JUST A QUICK PIECE
I SEE
INTERESTING! SOOO...
NUMBER TWO?
Sob!
2016 damian

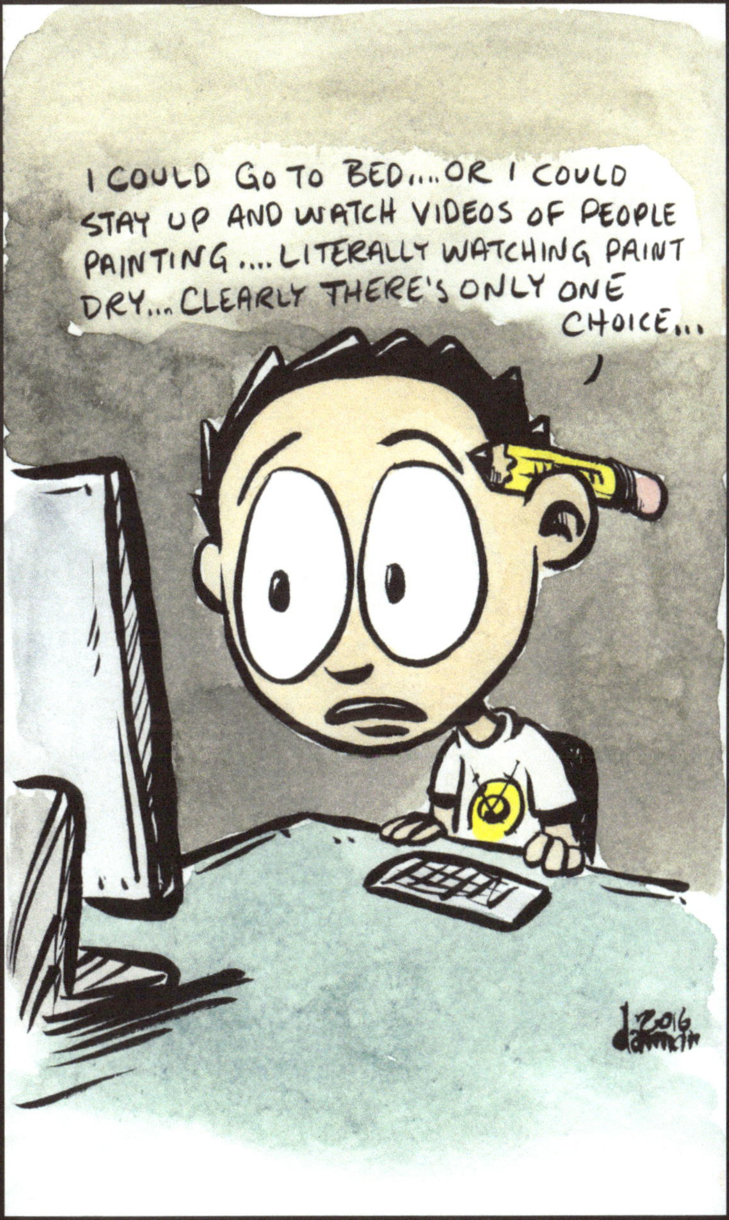
I COULD GO TO BED....OR I COULD STAY UP AND WATCH VIDEOS OF PEOPLE PAINTING....LITERALLY WATCHING PAINT DRY...CLEARLY THERE'S ONLY ONE CHOICE...

"Clearly..."

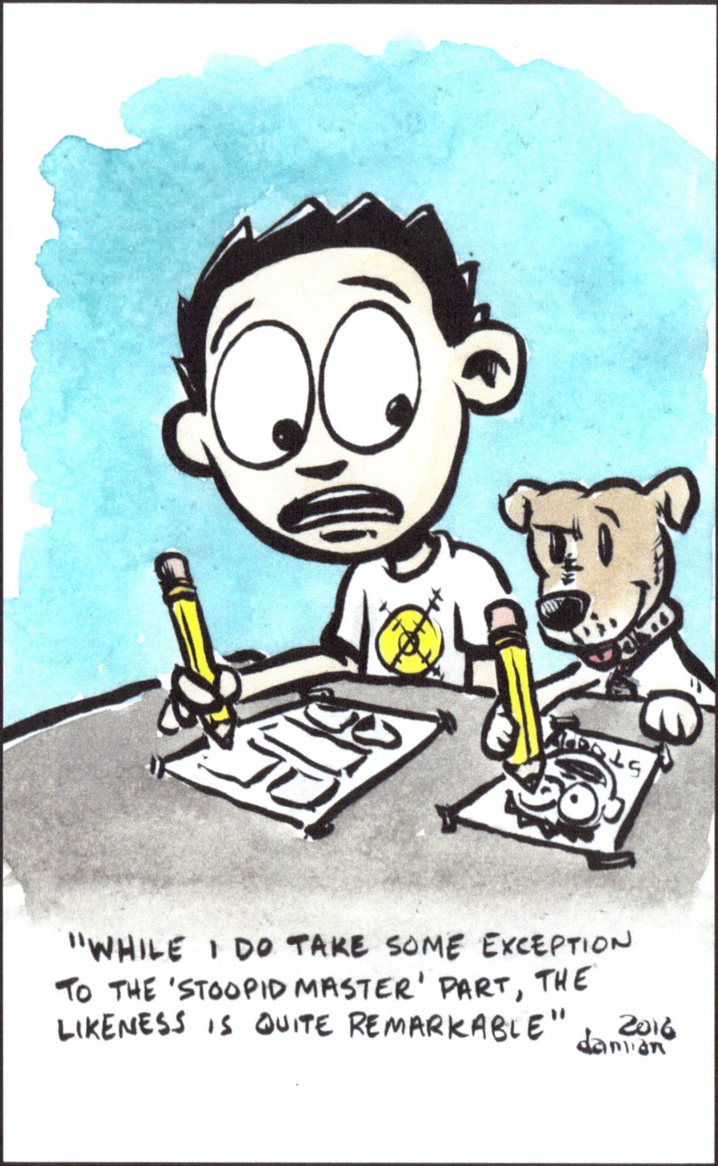
"WHILE I DO TAKE SOME EXCEPTION TO THE 'STOOPID MASTER' PART, THE LIKENESS IS QUITE REMARKABLE"
2016 damian

"Sketch artist"

comics about talking to your DOGS

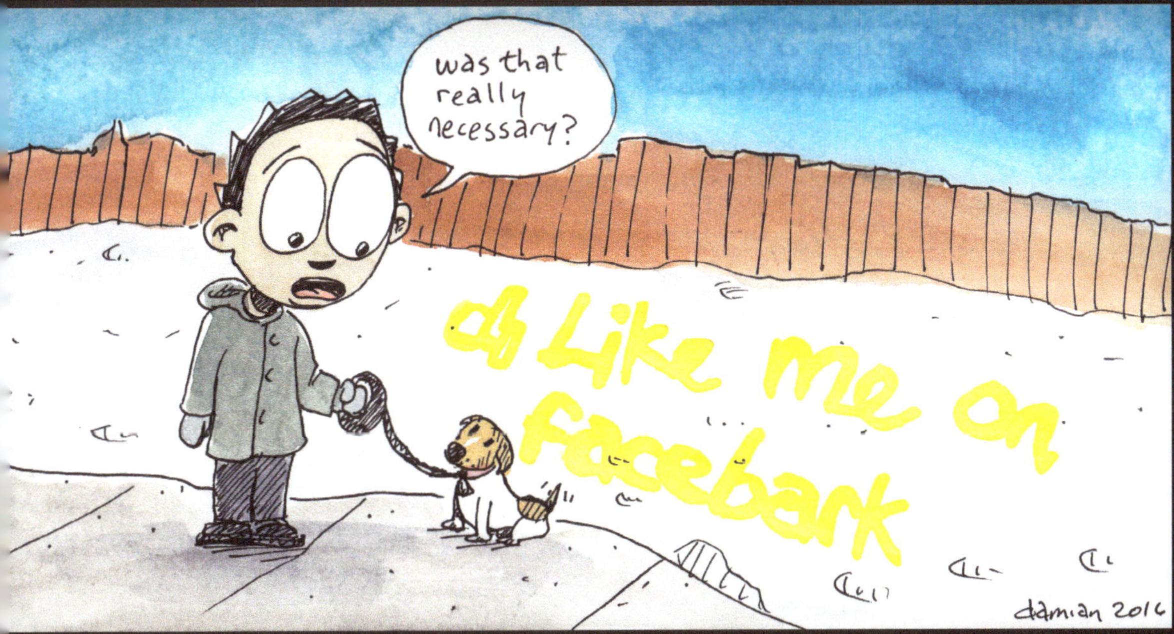
was that really necessary?
Like me on Facebark
damian 2016

"Snowcial networking"

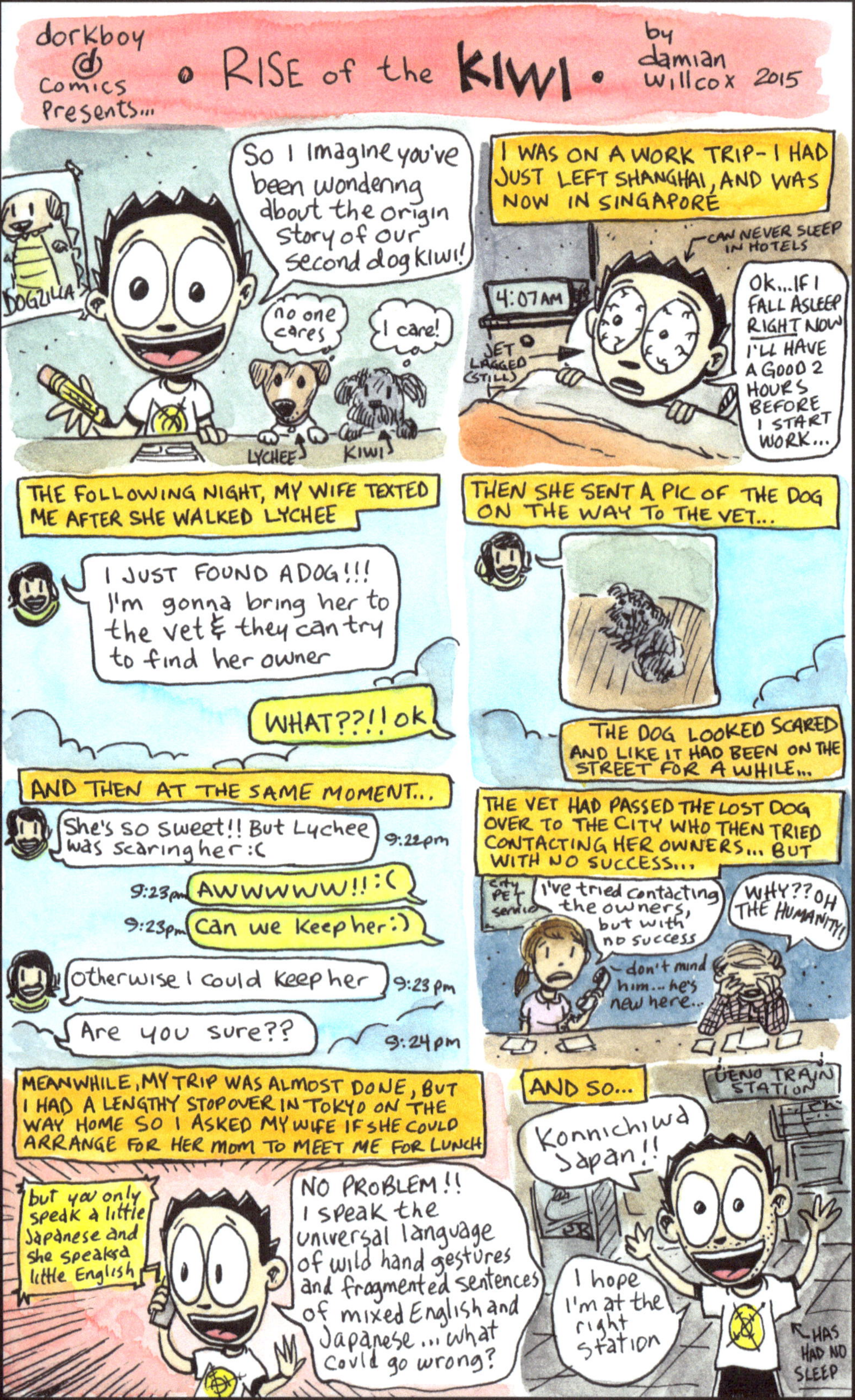
dorkboy comics presents...
• RISE of the KIWI •
by damian willcox 2015
So I imagine you've been wondering about the origin story of our second dog Kiwi!
DOGZILLA
no one cares
I care!
LYCHEE
KIWI
I WAS ON A WORK TRIP - I HAD JUST LEFT SHANGHAI, AND WAS NOW IN SINGAPORE
CAN NEVER SLEEP IN HOTELS
4:07 AM
JET LAGGED (STILL)
Ok... IF I FALL ASLEEP RIGHT NOW I'LL HAVE A GOOD 2 HOURS BEFORE I START WORK...
THE FOLLOWING NIGHT, MY WIFE TEXTED ME AFTER SHE WALKED LYCHEE
I JUST FOUND A DOG!!! I'm gonna bring her to the vet & they can try to find her owner
WHAT??!! ok
THEN SHE SENT A PIC OF THE DOG ON THE WAY TO THE VET...
THE DOG LOOKED SCARED AND LIKE IT HAD BEEN ON THE STREET FOR A WHILE...
AND THEN AT THE SAME MOMENT...
She's so sweet!! But Lychee was scaring her :(
9:22pm
9:23pm
AWWWWW!! :(
9:23pm
Can we keep her :)
otherwise I could keep her
9:23 pm
Are you sure??
9:24 pm
THE VET HAD PASSED THE LOST DOG OVER TO THE CITY WHO THEN TRIED CONTACTING HER OWNERS... BUT WITH NO SUCCESS...
City PET Service
I've tried contacting the owners, but with no success
WHY?? OH THE HUMANITY!!
don't mind him... he's new here...
MEANWHILE, MY TRIP WAS ALMOST DONE, BUT I HAD A LENGTHY STOPOVER IN TOKYO ON THE WAY HOME SO I ASKED MY WIFE IF SHE COULD ARRANGE FOR HER MOM TO MEET ME FOR LUNCH
but you only speak a little Japanese and she speaks a little English
NO PROBLEM!! I speak the universal language of wild hand gestures and fragmented sentences of mixed English and Japanese... what could go wrong?
AND SO...
UENO TRAIN STATION
Konnichiwa Japan!!
I hope I'm at the right station
HAS HAD NO SLEEP

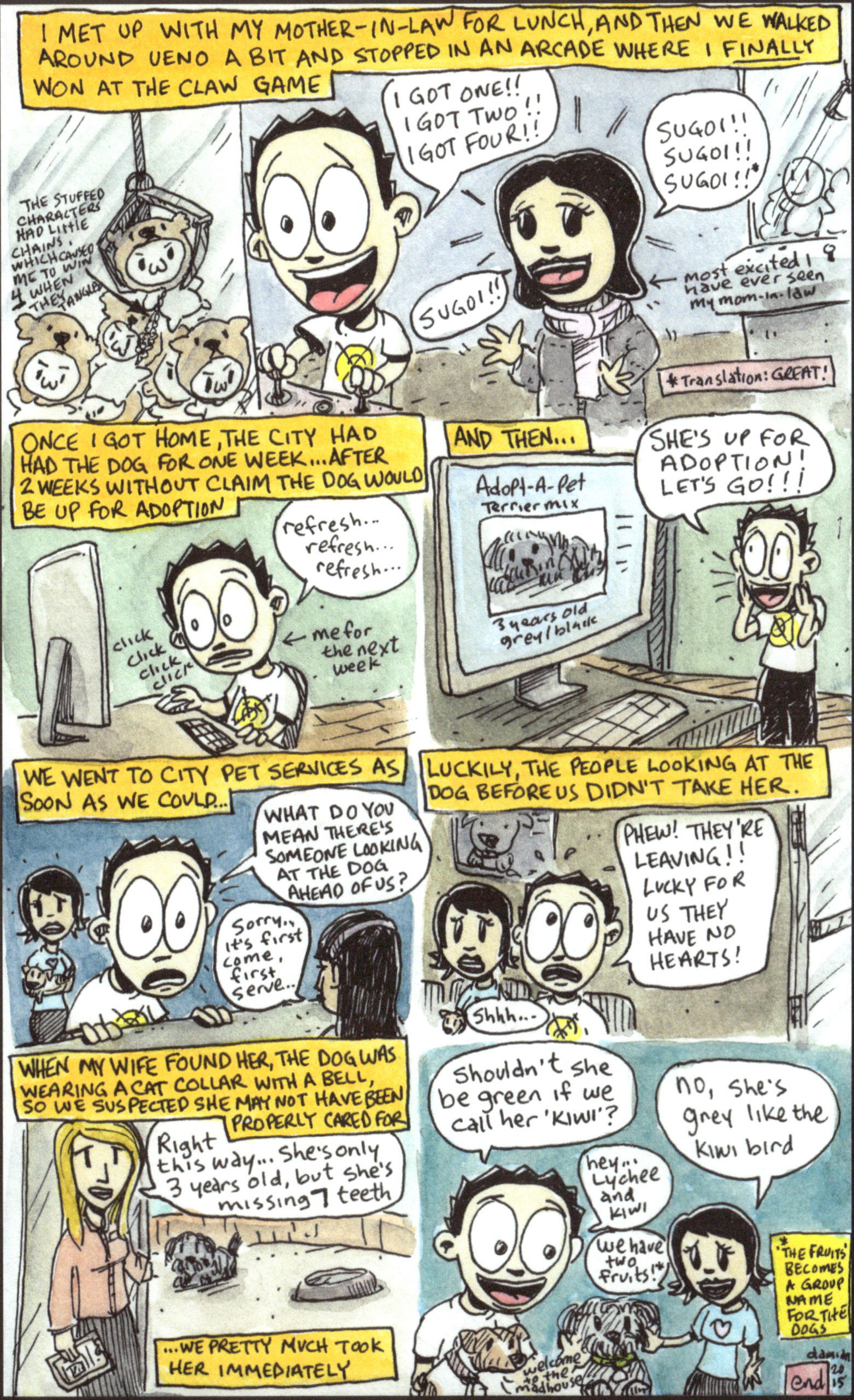
I MET UP WITH MY MOTHER-IN-LAW FOR LUNCH, AND THEN WE WALKED AROUND UENO A BIT AND STOPPED IN AN ARCADE WHERE I FINALLY WON AT THE CLAW GAME
THE STUFFED CHARACTERS HAD LITTLE CHAINS, WHICH CAUSED ME TO WIN 4 WHEN THEY TANGLED
I GOT ONE!! I GOT TWO!! I GOT FOUR!!
SUGOI!! SUGOI!! SUGOI!!*
SUGOI!!
most excited I have ever seen my mom-in-law
*Translation: GREAT!
ONCE I GOT HOME, THE CITY HAD HAD THE DOG FOR ONE WEEK... AFTER 2 WEEKS WITHOUT CLAIM THE DOG WOULD BE UP FOR ADOPTION
refresh... refresh... refresh...
click click click click
me for the next week
AND THEN...
Adopt-A-Pet
Terrier mix
3 years old grey/black
SHE'S UP FOR ADOPTION! LET'S GO!!!
WE WENT TO CITY PET SERVICES AS SOON AS WE COULD...
WHAT DO YOU MEAN THERE'S SOMEONE LOOKING AT THE DOG AHEAD OF US?
Sorry.. it's first come, first serve...
LUCKILY, THE PEOPLE LOOKING AT THE DOG BEFORE US DIDN'T TAKE HER.
PHEW! THEY'RE LEAVING!! LUCKY FOR US THEY HAVE NO HEARTS!
Shhh...
WHEN MY WIFE FOUND HER, THE DOG WAS WEARING A CAT COLLAR WITH A BELL, SO WE SUSPECTED SHE MAY NOT HAVE BEEN PROPERLY CARED FOR
Right this way... She's only 3 years old, but she's missing 7 teeth
...WE PRETTY MUCH TOOK HER IMMEDIATELY
Shouldn't she be green if we call her 'KIWI'?
no, she's grey like the Kiwi bird
hey... Lychee and Kiwi
We have two Fruits!*
*'THE FRUITS' BECOMES A GROUP NAME FOR THE DOGS
welcome to the madhouse
damian 2015
end

dorkboy @ comics presents... · · · · · · · by damian
"AUTUMN-ATIC APPROVAL" willcox 2014

hi everyone, I'm here to talk about the best time of the year!

Hanukkah?

no

Chanukah?

no...

Veronica?

no, that's not even...

FALL!!

You could have given a better hint...

Lychee, did you know that Fall is the only season that is a noun AND a verb?

oh... you mean like spring? dummy...

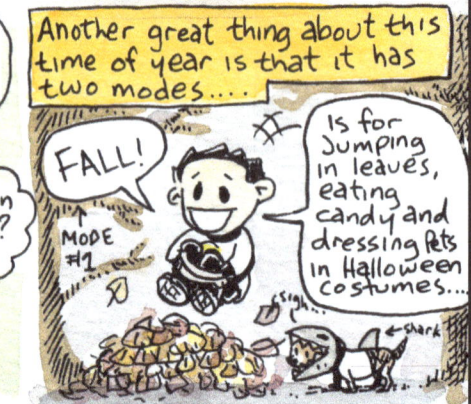

Another great thing about this time of year is that it has two modes....

FALL!

MODE #1

Is for jumping in leaves, eating candy and dressing pets in Halloween costumes...

←shark

...and then there's the dignified 'AUTUMN'

mode #2

...it's like the fancy evening wear counterpart to Fall's turtleneck where you eat pumpkin pie with a fork!

as opposed to?

IN FACT... IT SHOULD REALLY BE CALLED 'AUSUMN'...THAT'S HOW GREAT IT IS!

are we done yet?

Autumn doesn't walk around like summer + winter saying "look at me and my solstice"!!

ok, got it... Fall is the best. NOW, back to my original request...

Can you hurry up and let me outside so that I can create some autumn colours of my own, if you know what I mean...

yuck...

end

damian 20 14

comics about
EVERYTHING ELSE

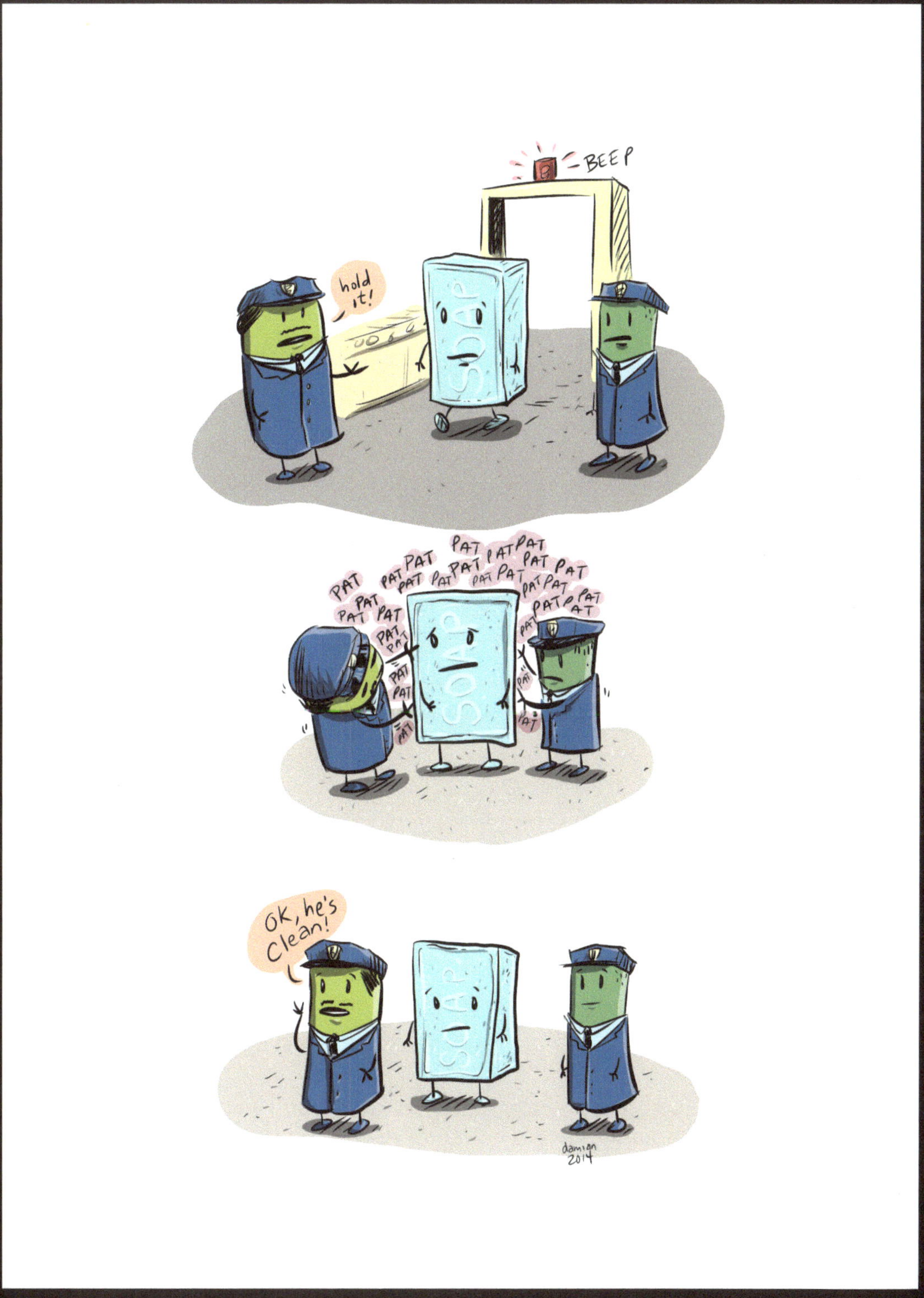
BEEP
hold it!
SOAP
PAT PAT PAT PAT PAT PAT PAT PAT PAT PAT PAT PAT PAT PAT PAT PAT PAT PAT PAT PAT PAT
Ok, he's Clean!
damian 2014

grab!
tie
tie
CISS
the
KOOK
stir
stir
stir

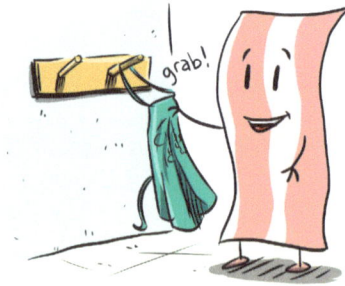

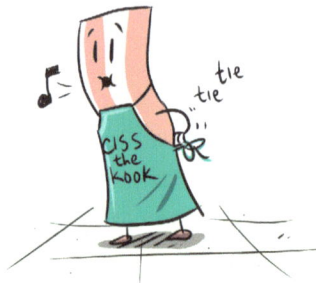

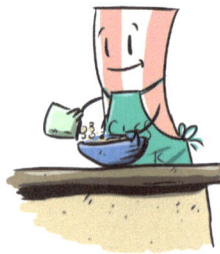

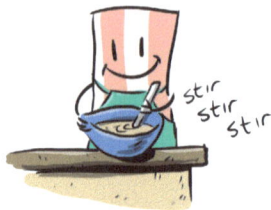

pour pour
doot de doot de
oh, hey! Check it out...
I'm bacon!

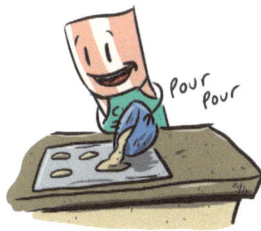

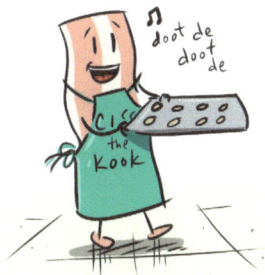

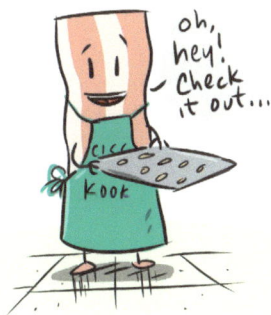

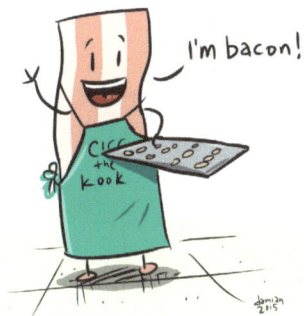

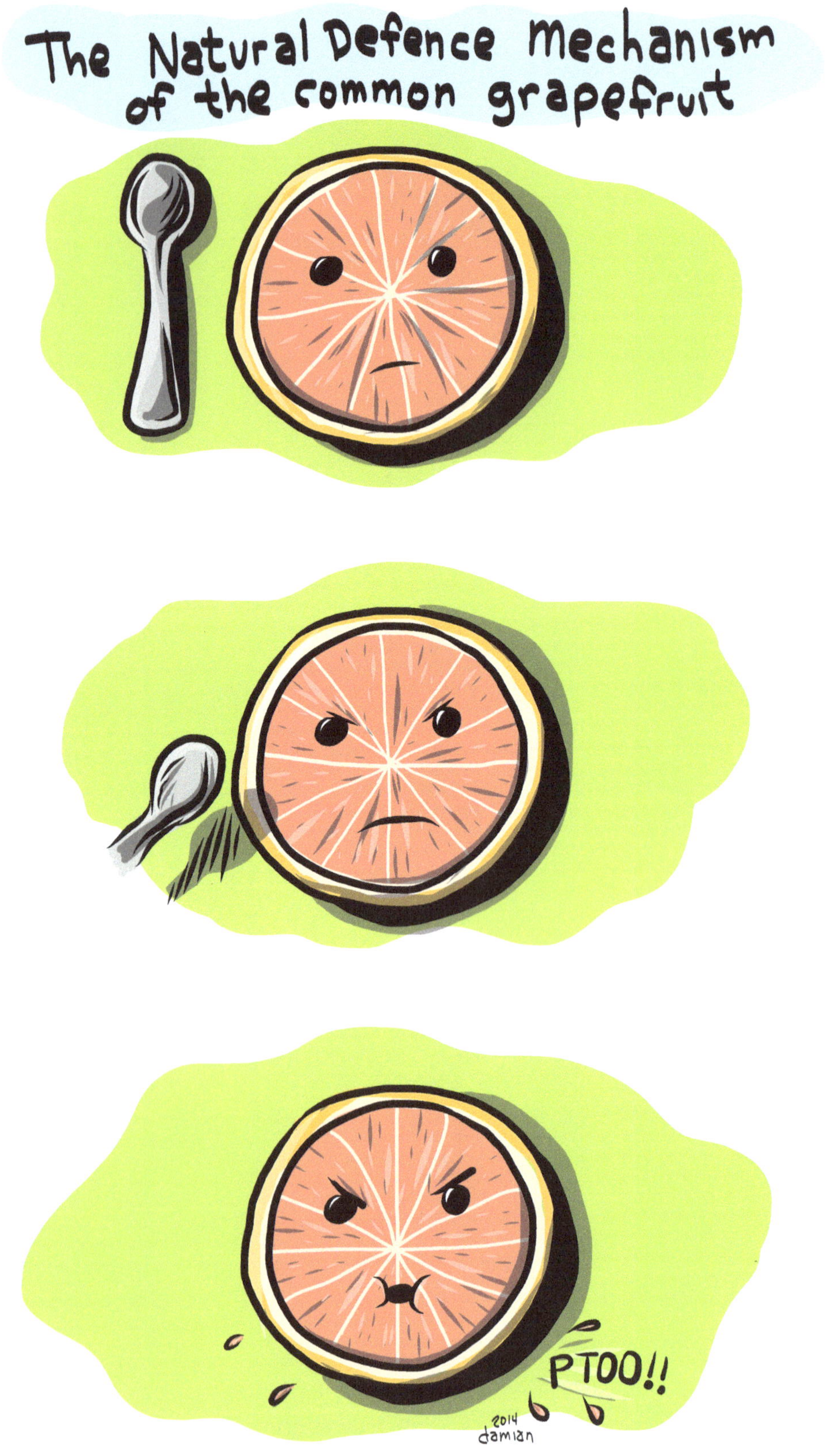
The Natural Defence Mechanism of the common grapefruit
PTOO!!
2014 damian

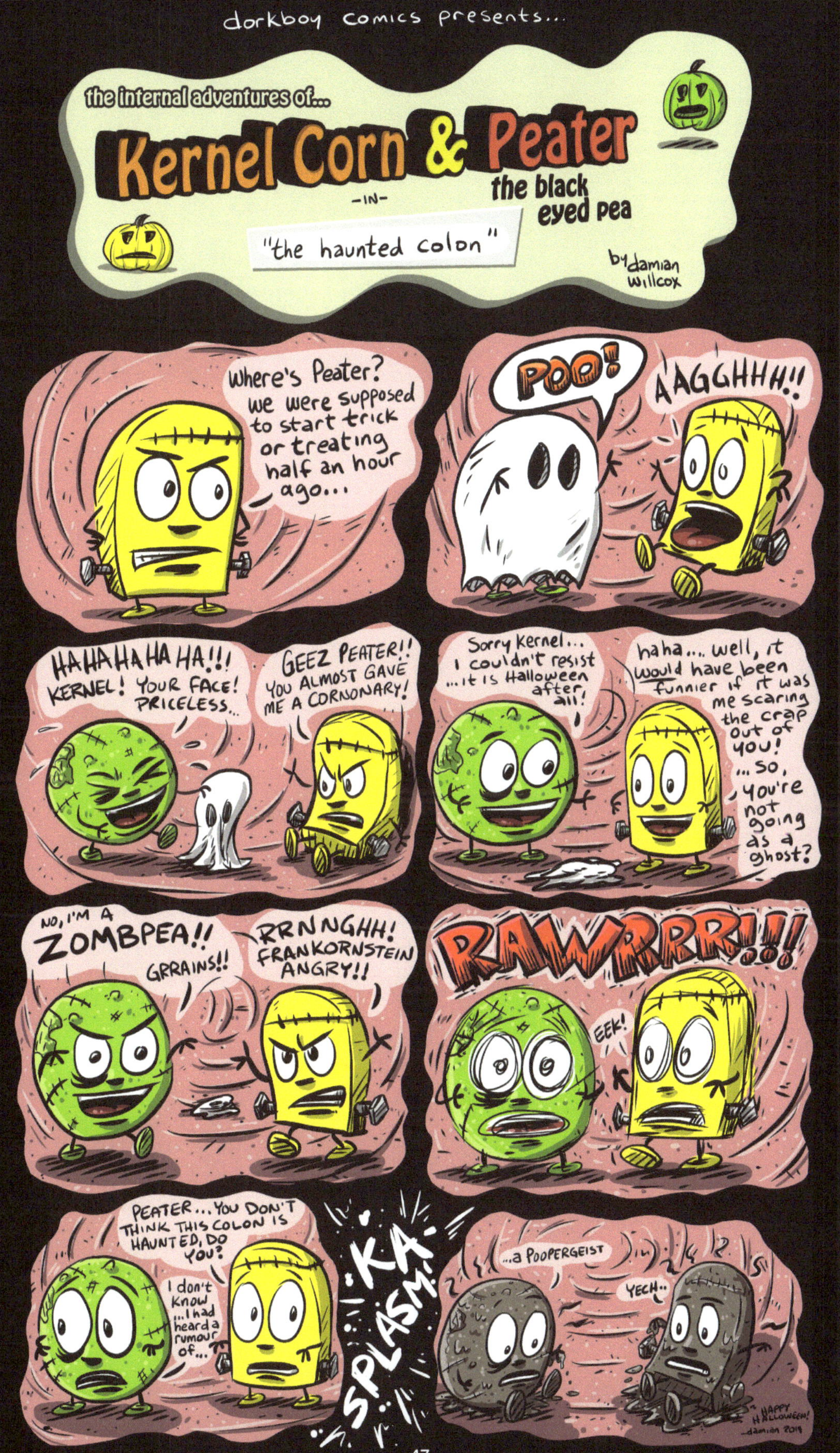
dorkboy comics presents...
the internal adventures of...
Kernel Corn & Peater the black eyed pea
-IN-
"the haunted colon"
by damian willcox
Where's Peater? we were supposed to start trick or treating half an hour ago...
POO!
AAGGHHH!!
HAHAHAHAHA!!! KERNEL! YOUR FACE! PRICELESS...
GEEZ PEATER!! YOU ALMOST GAVE ME A CORNONARY!
Sorry Kernel... I couldn't resist ...it is Halloween after all!
haha... well, it would have been funnier if it was me scaring the crap out of you! ...So, you're not going as a ghost?
NO, I'M A ZOMBPEA!! GRRAINS!!
RRNNGHH! FRANKORNSTEIN ANGRY!!
RAWRRR!!!
EEK!
PEATER... YOU DON'T THINK THIS COLON IS HAUNTED, DO YOU?
I don't know ...I had heard a rumour of...
KA SPLASM!
...a POOPERGEIST
YECH..
HAPPY HALLOWEEN! damian 2019

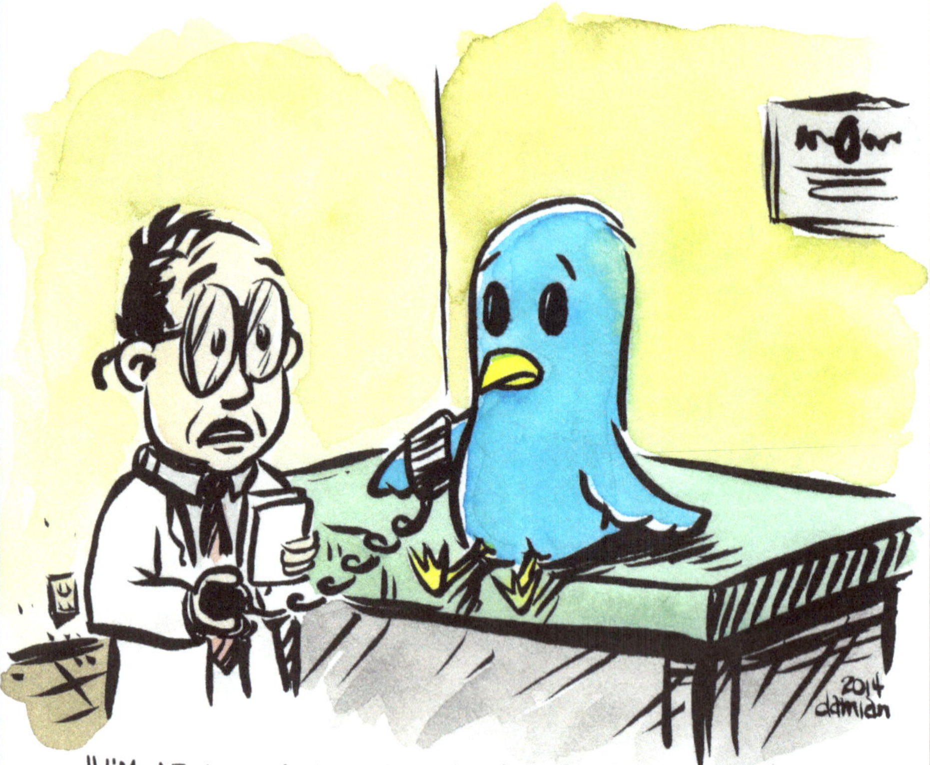
2014
damian

"I'M AFRAID YOU'VE GOT HIGH BIRD PRESSURE"

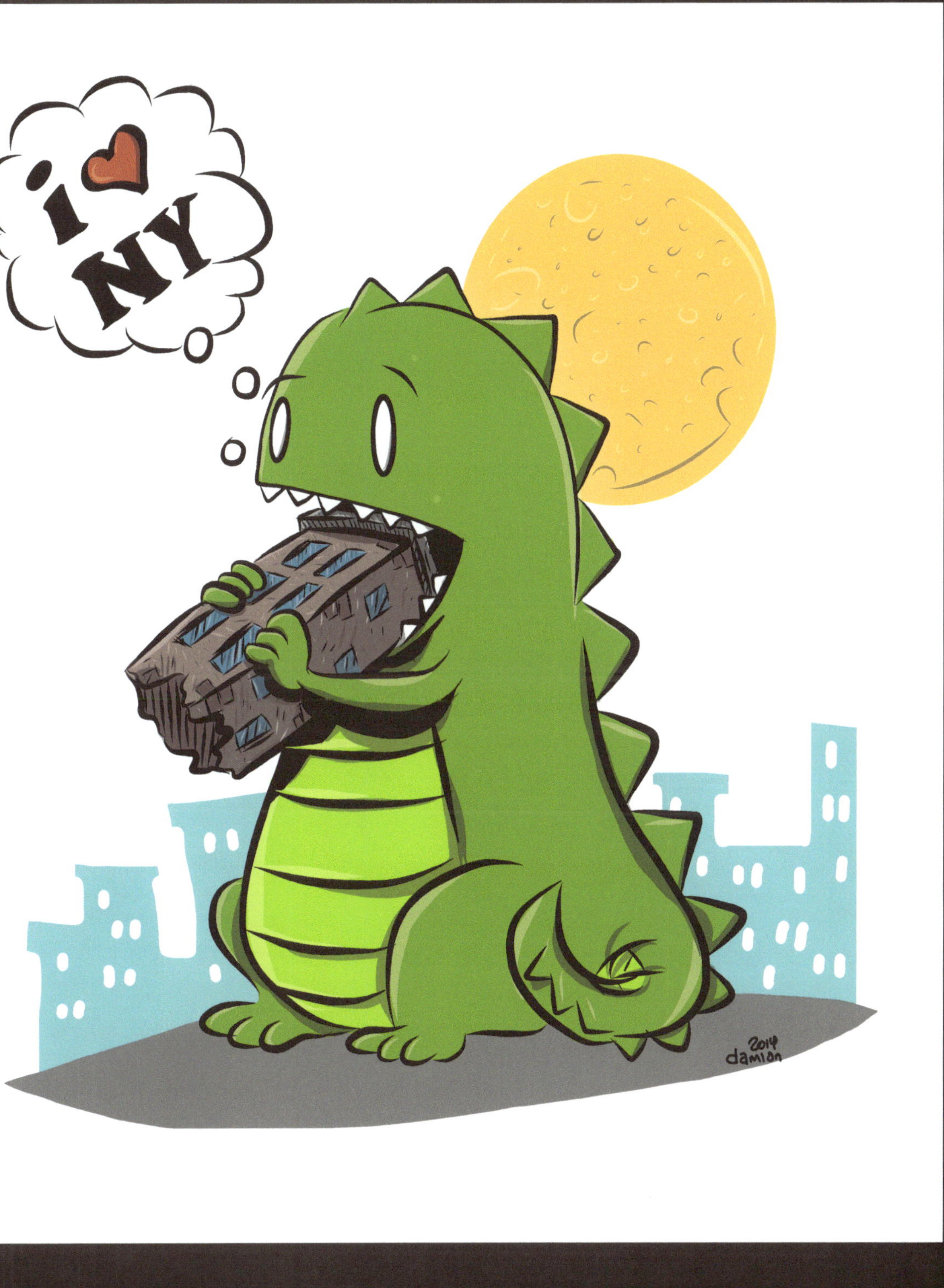
i ♥ NY
2014
damion

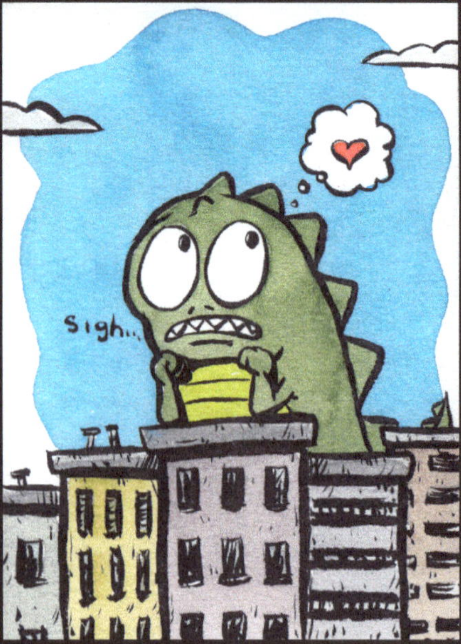
Sigh...

"Godzilla vs Unrequited Love"

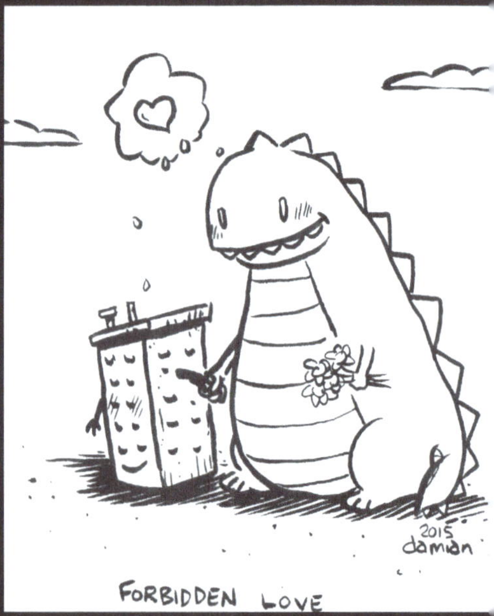
2015
damian
FORBIDDEN LOVE

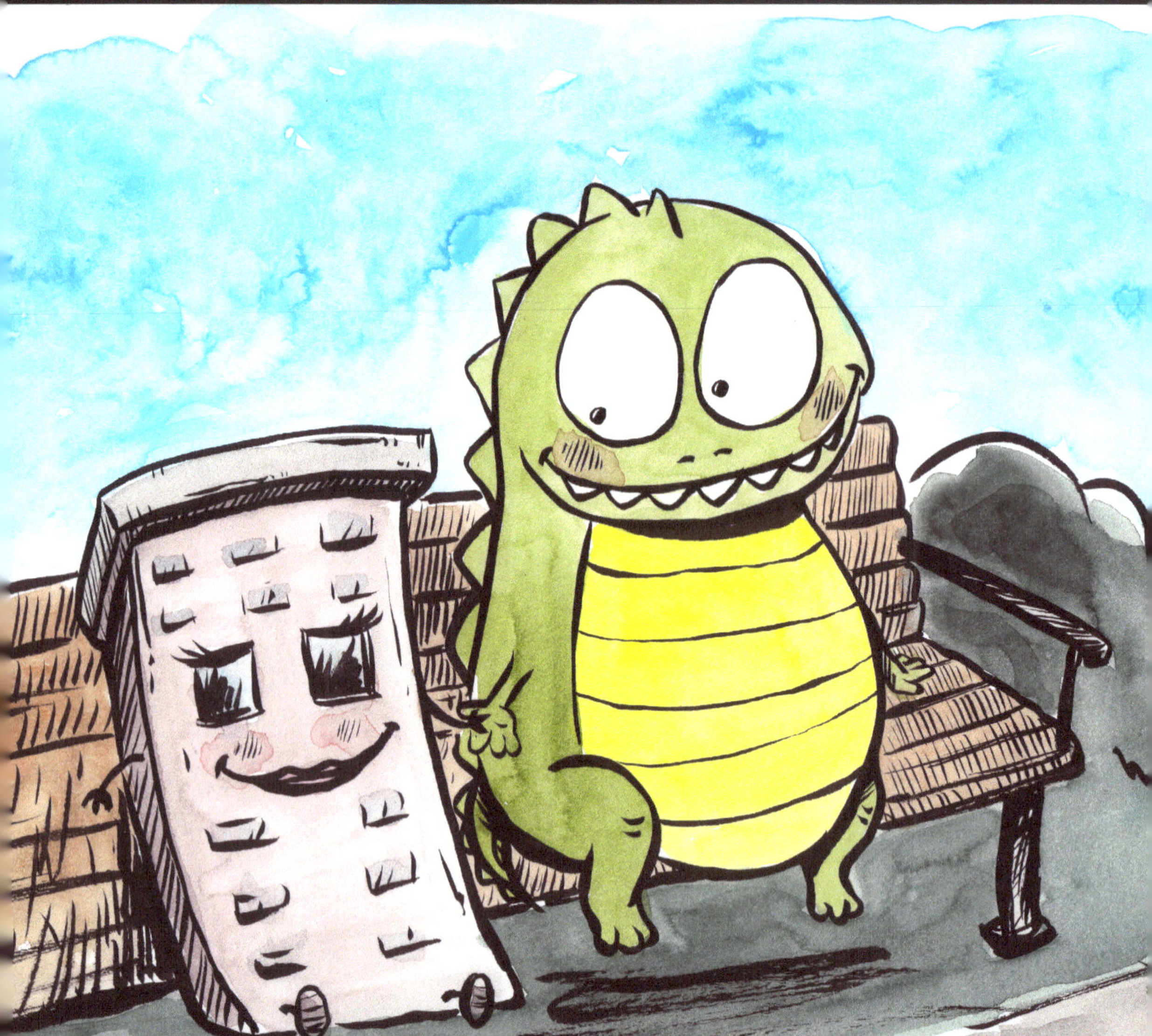

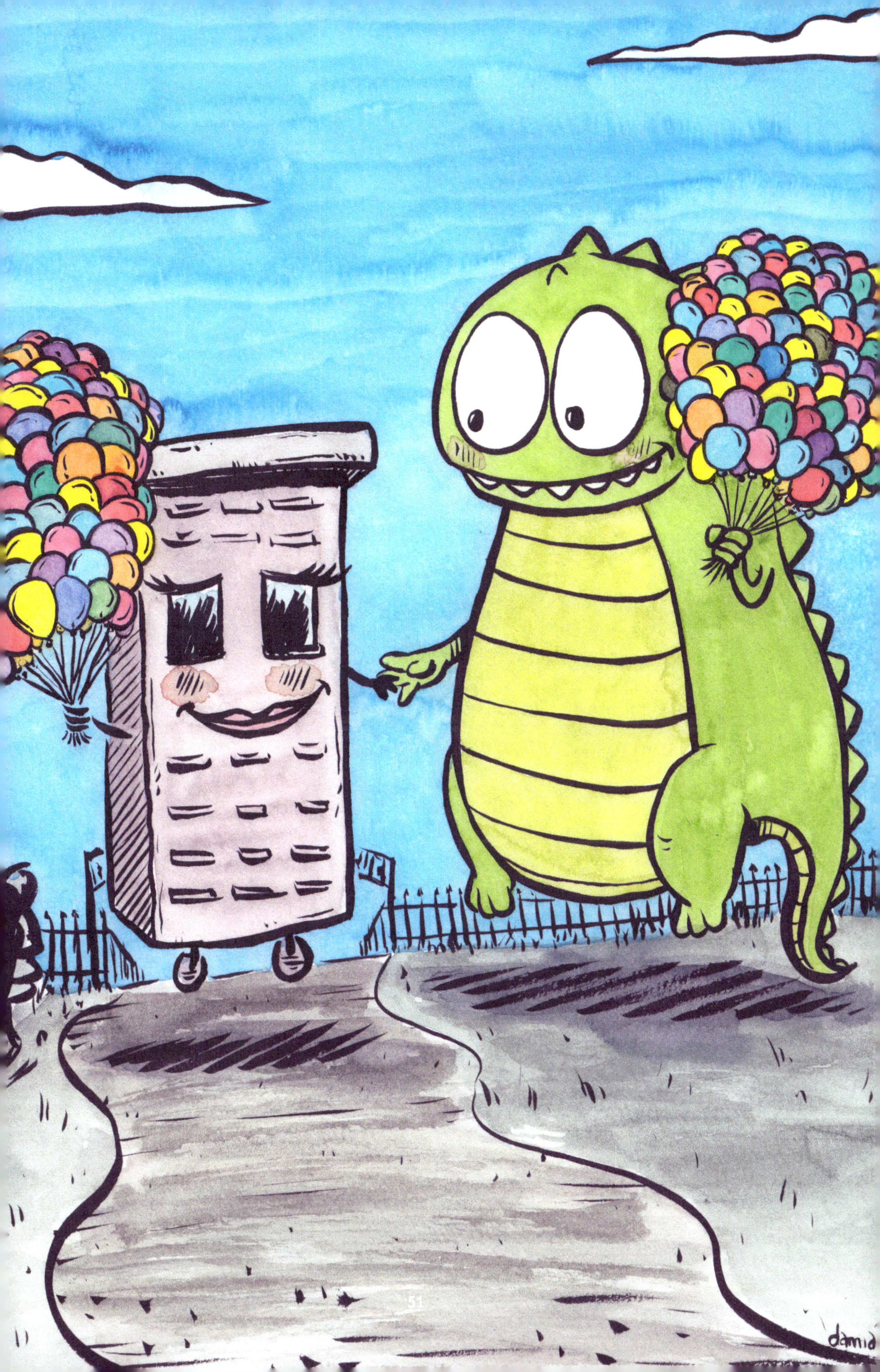
dàmia

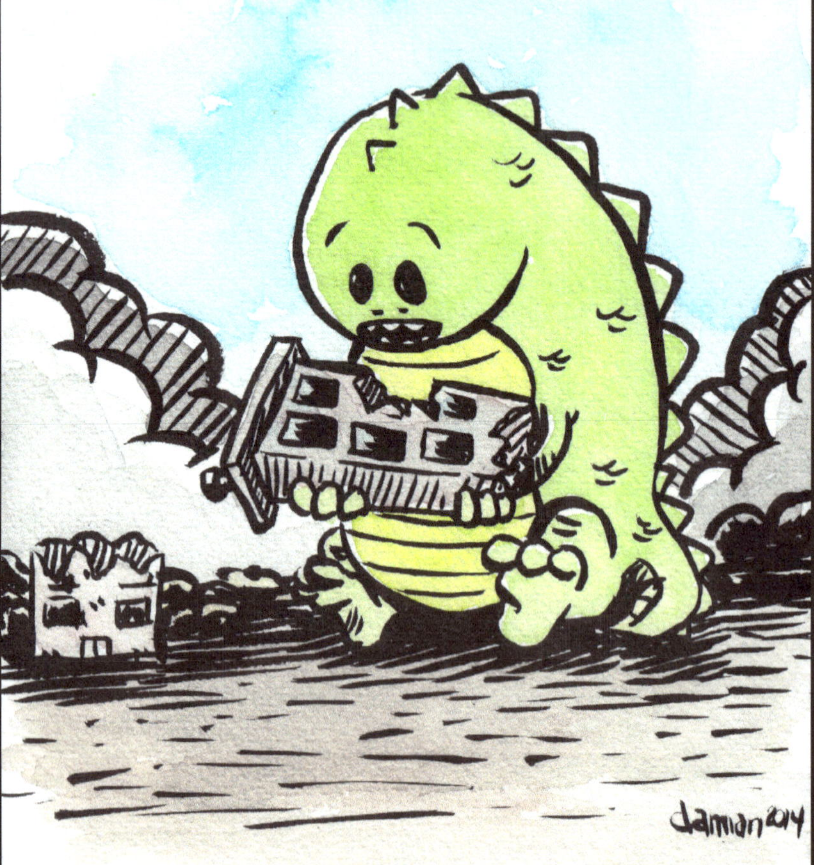
damian 2014

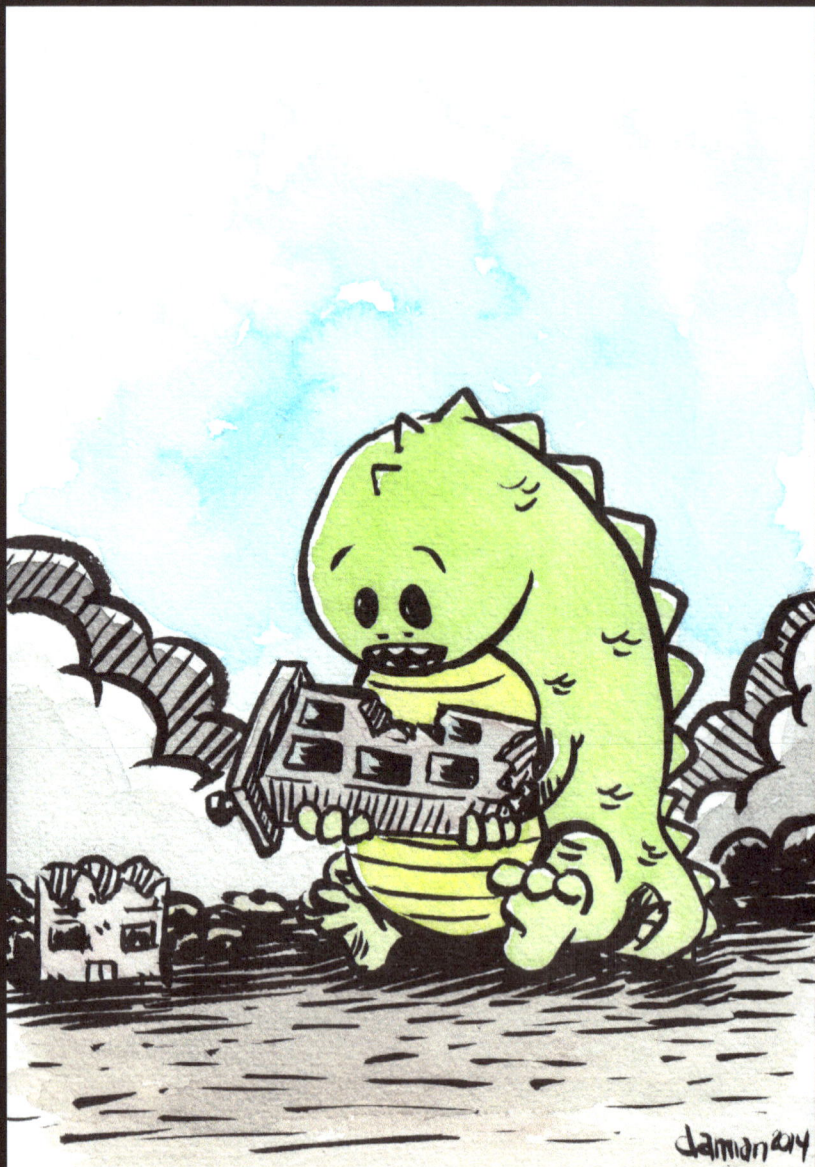

"ugh, it has seeds!"

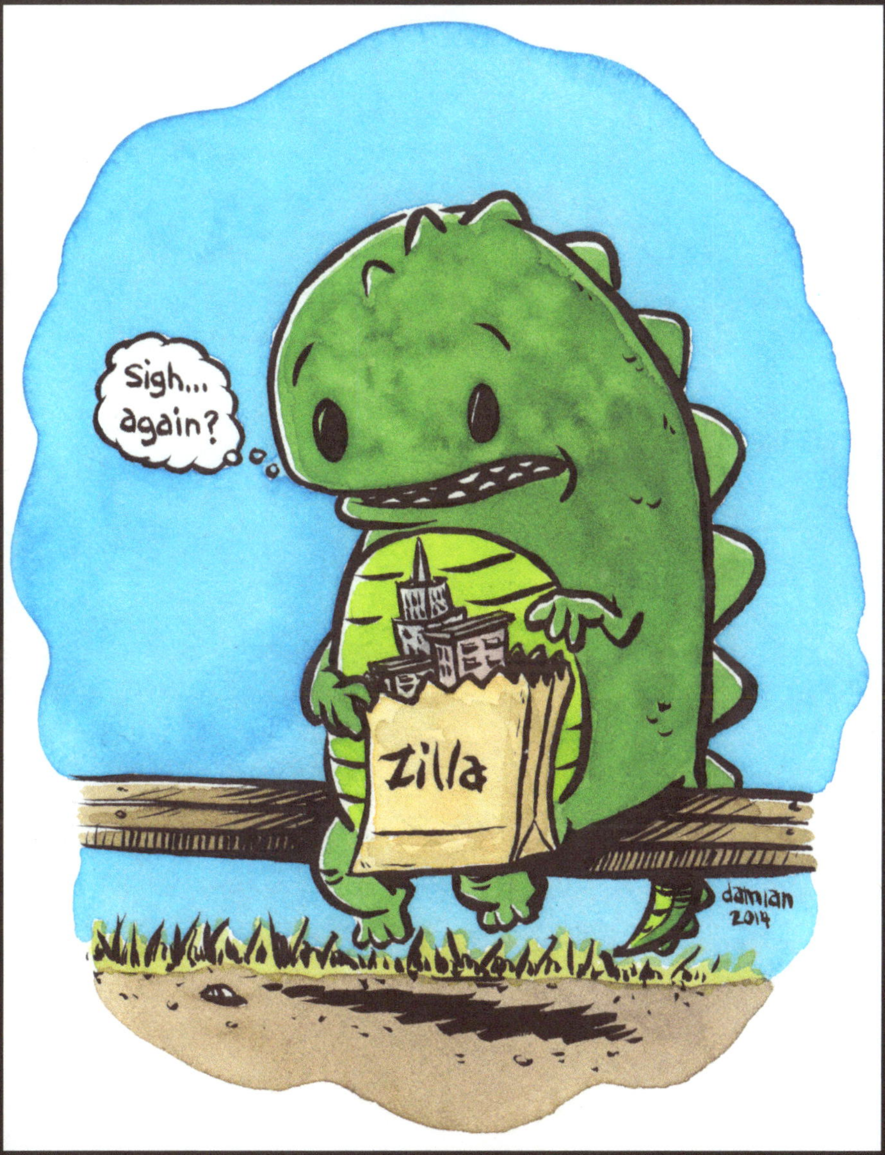
Sigh...
again?
Zilla
damian
2014

"Lunch in the city"

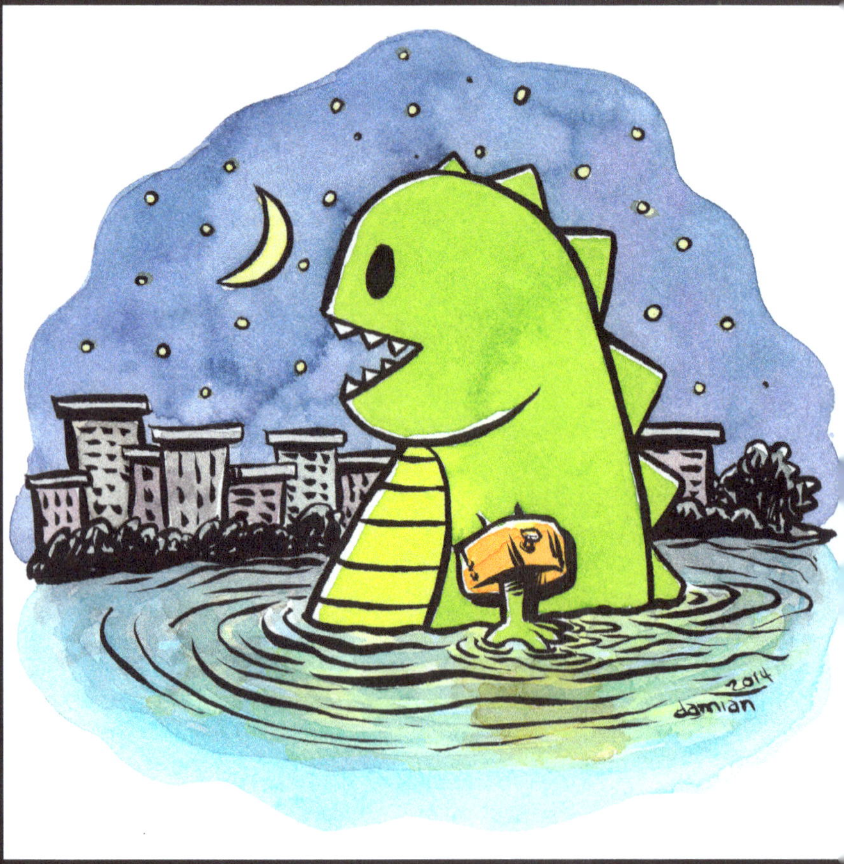
2014
damian

"Water wings & late night dreams"

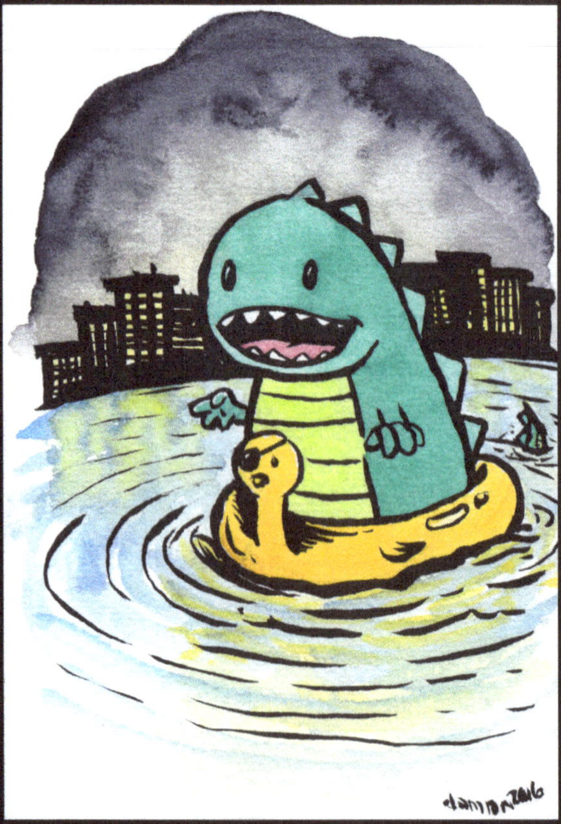

"Thanks for the memories, Tokyo."

next page: "Waiting"

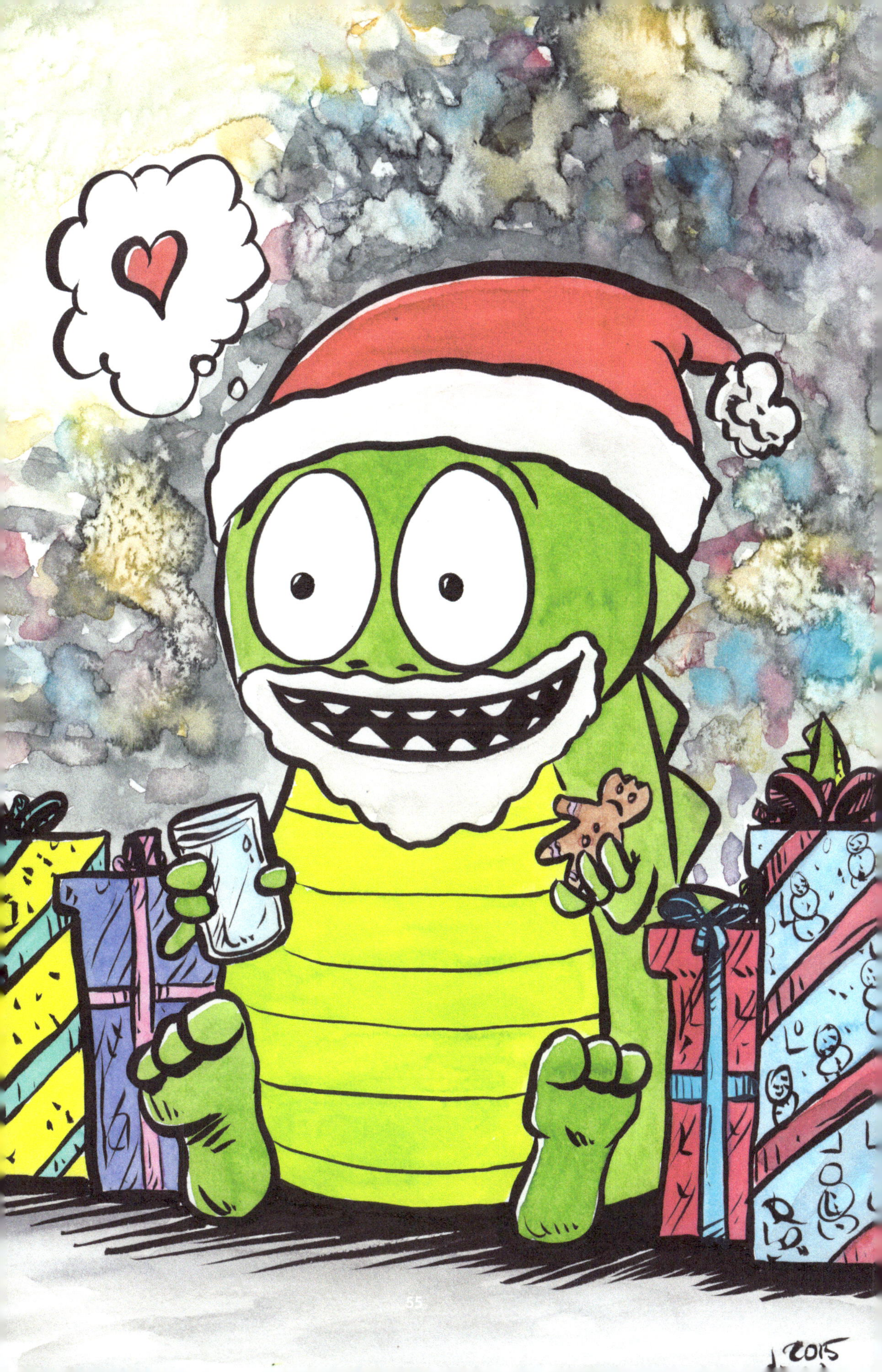

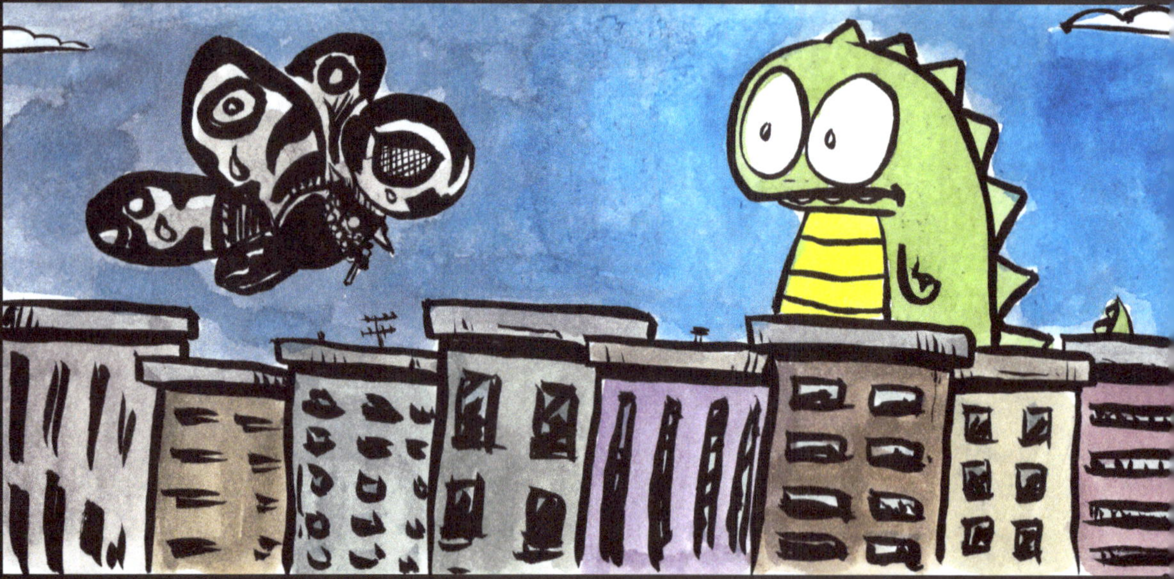

"Godzilla vs Gothra"

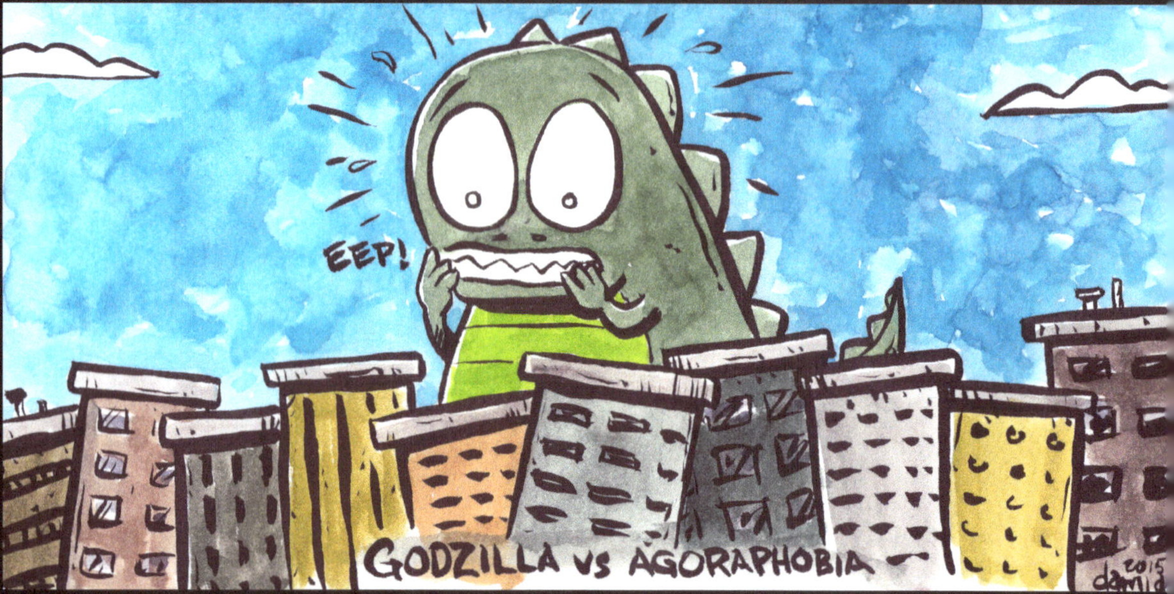
EEP!
GODZILLA VS AGORAPHOBIA
2015
david

"Godzilla vs Agoraphobia"

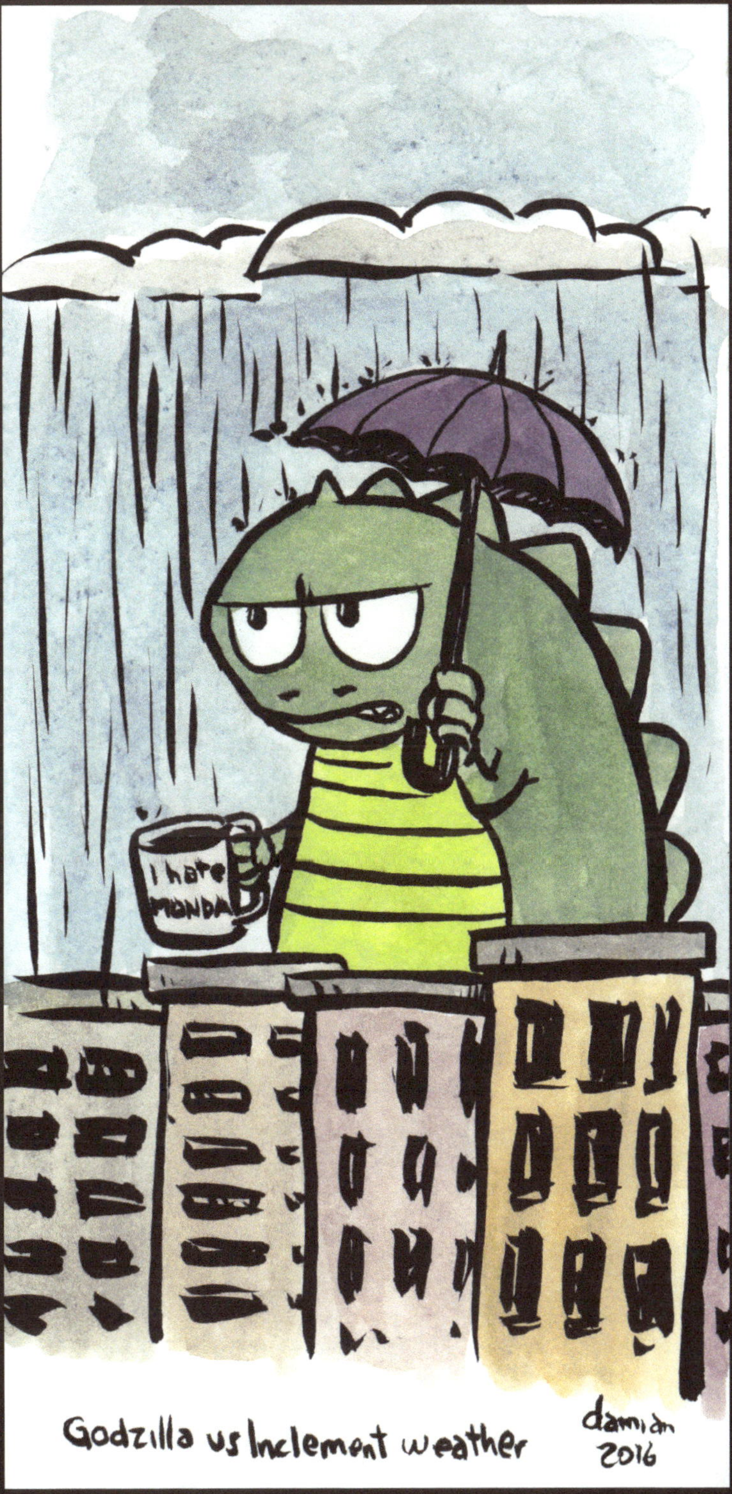
I hate MONDA
Godzilla vs Inclement weather
damian 2016

"Godzilla vs Inclement Weather"

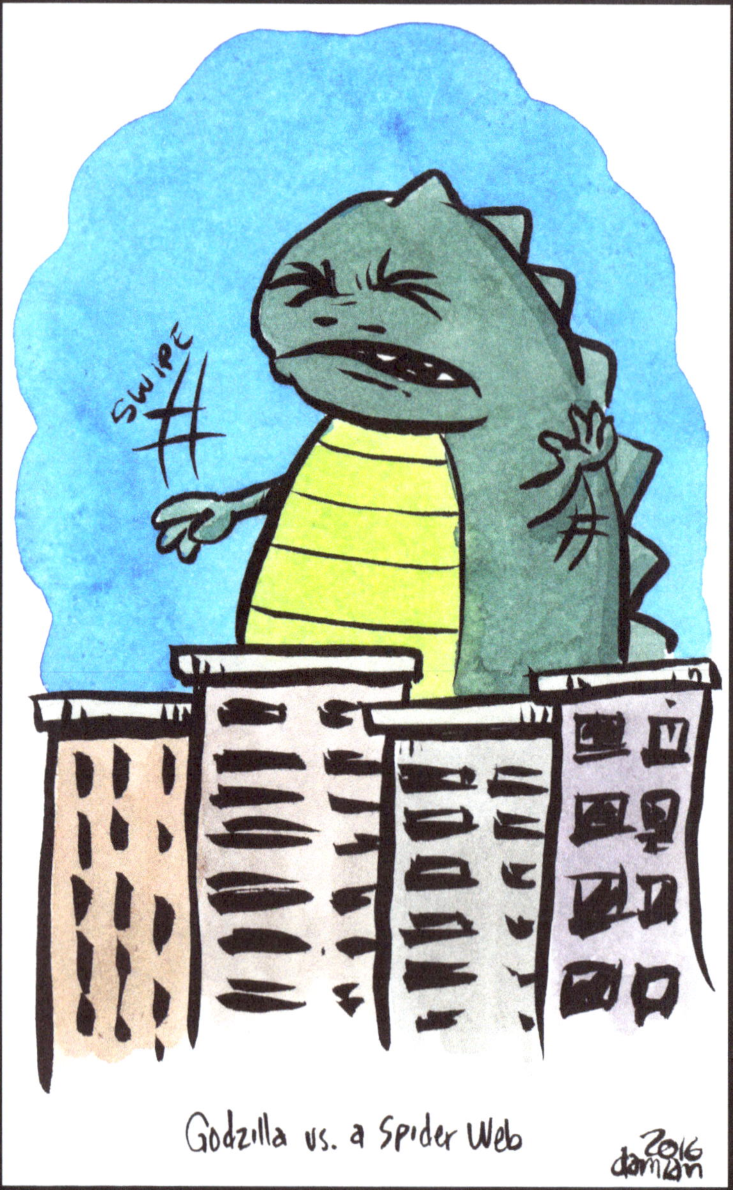
SWIPE
Godzilla vs. a Spider Web
2016
damian

"Godzilla vs a Spider Web"

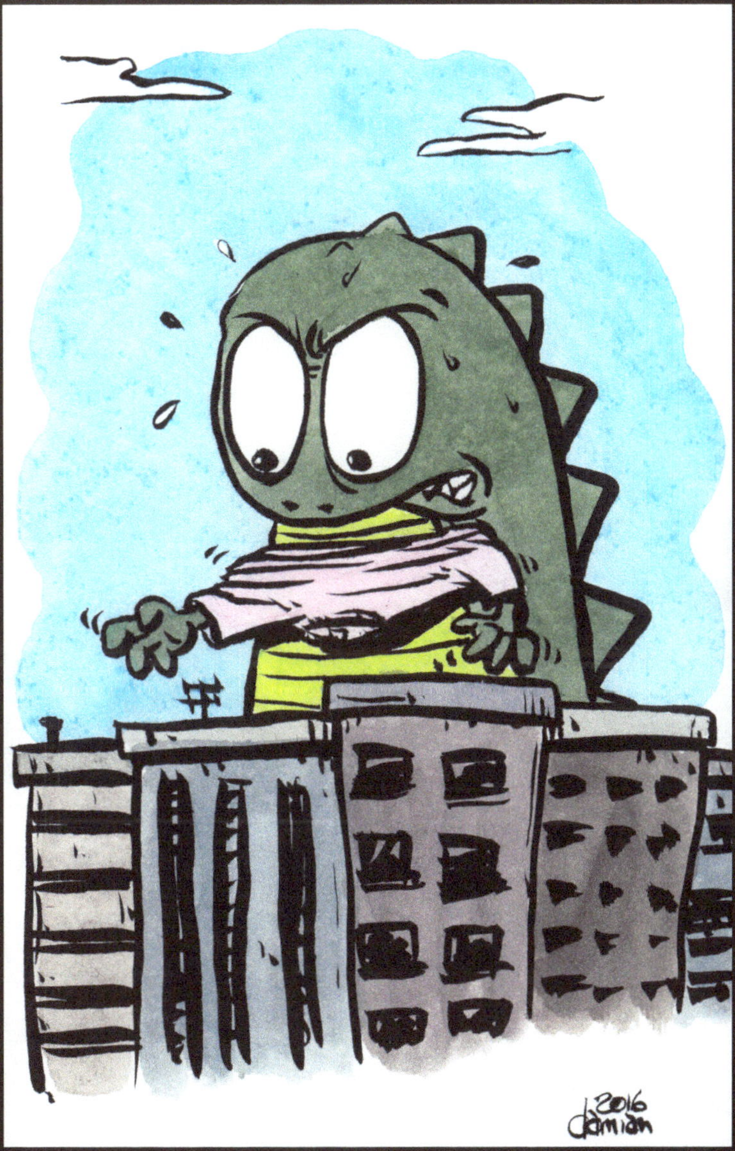
2016
damian

"Godzilla vs a Hot Wash Cycle (with a red sock)"

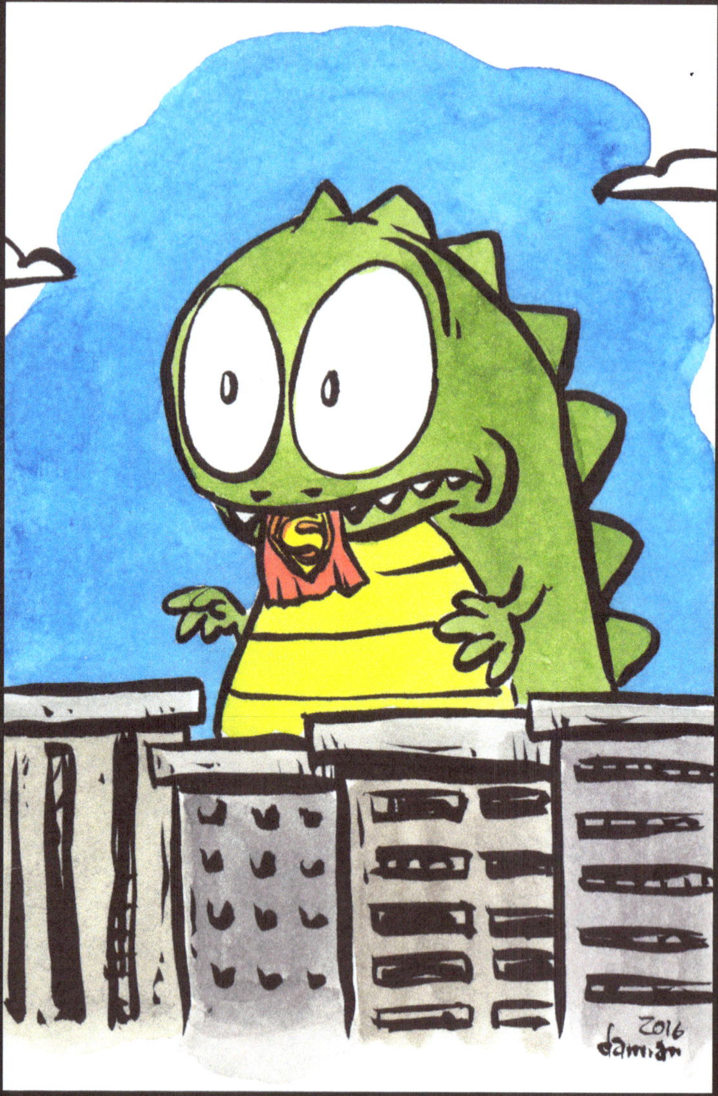
2016
damian

"Yawning Godzilla vs Metropolis"

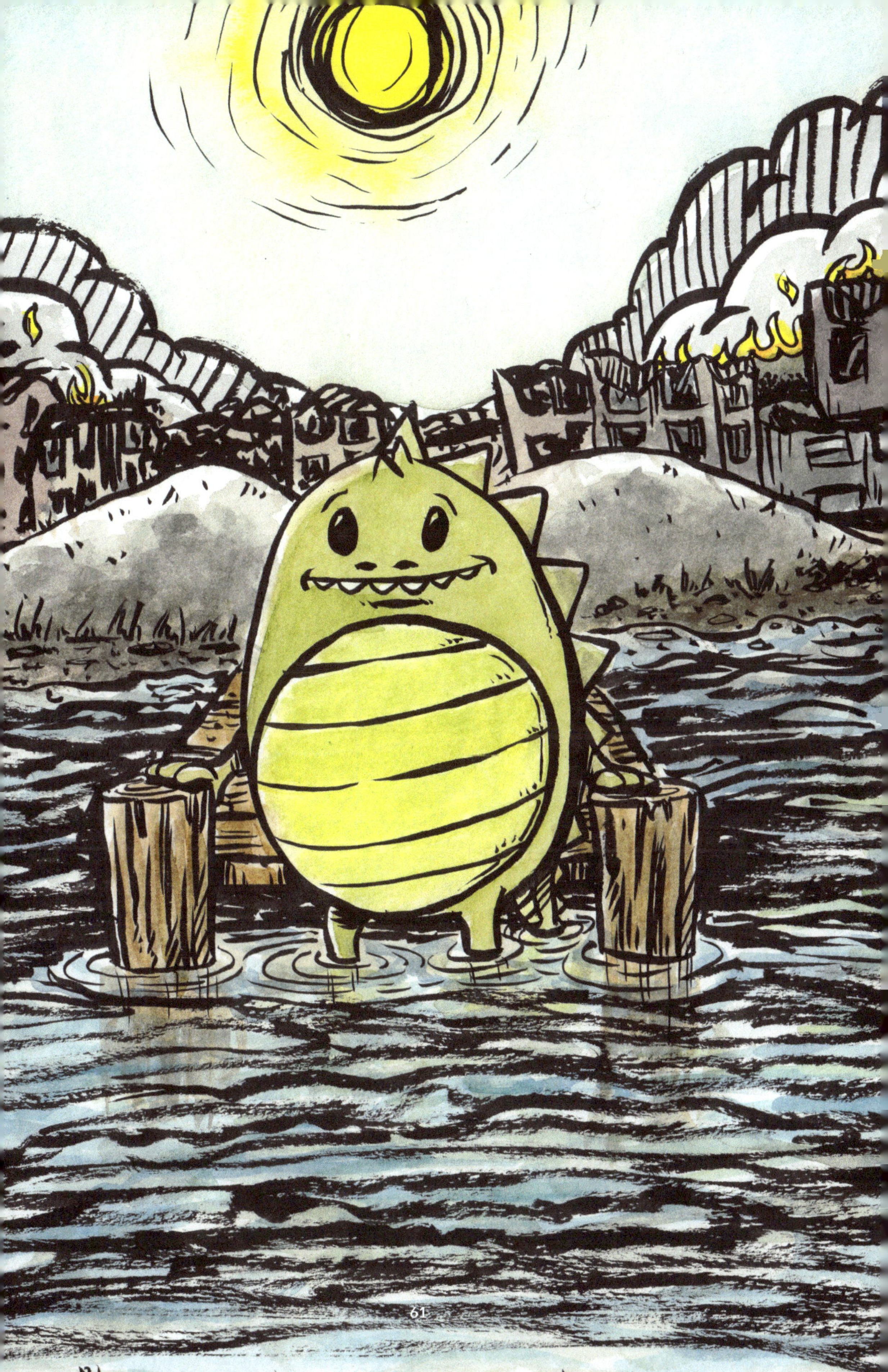

"it's a bird! it's a pla...OMG!!!"

next page: " Godzilla vs Canada'

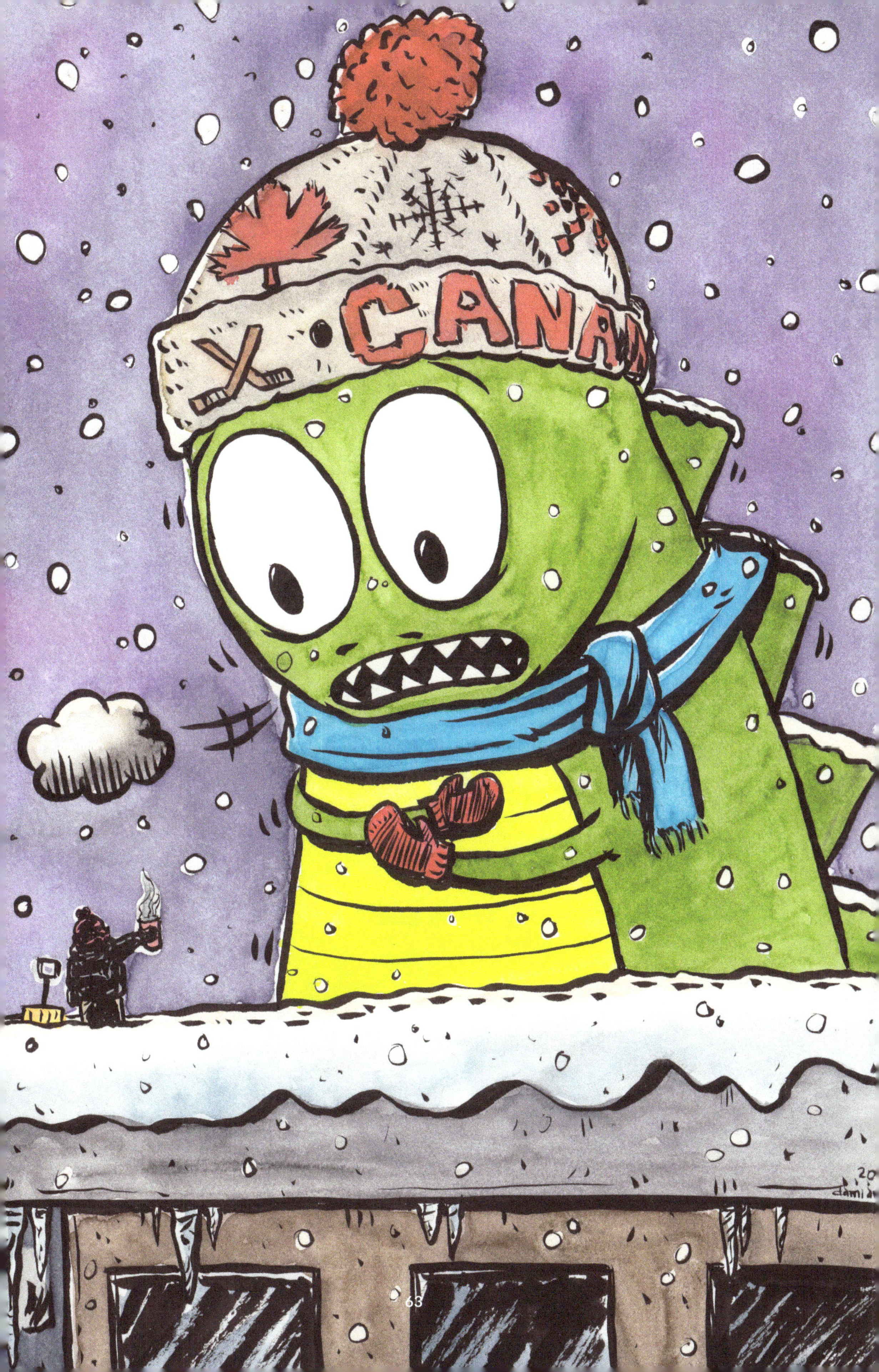
CANA

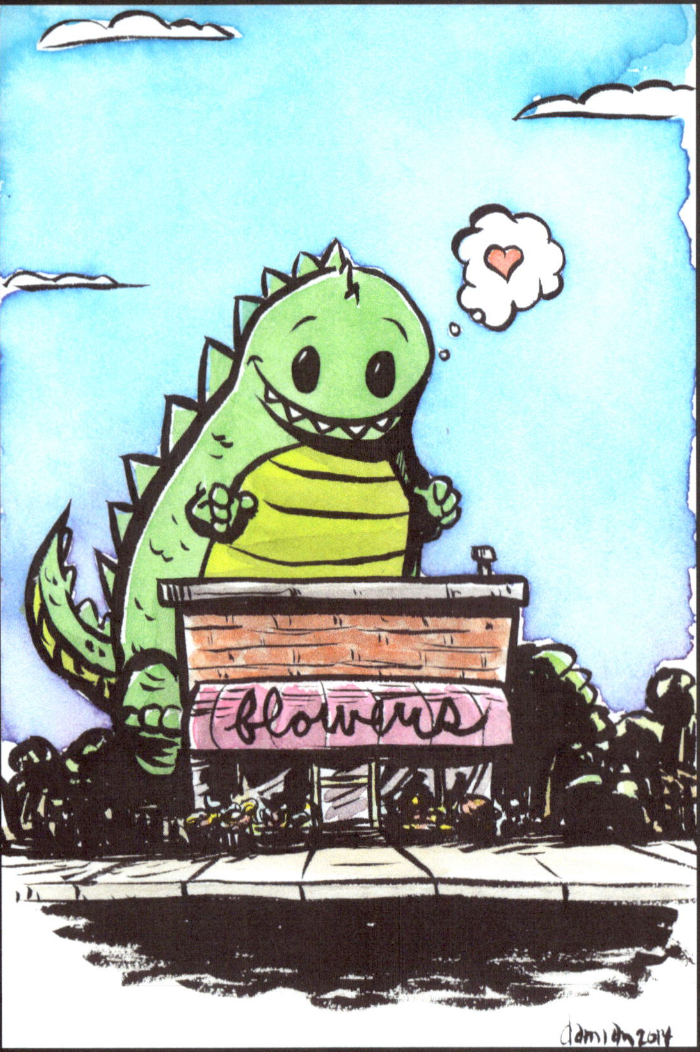
flowers
damian 2014

"floralzilla"

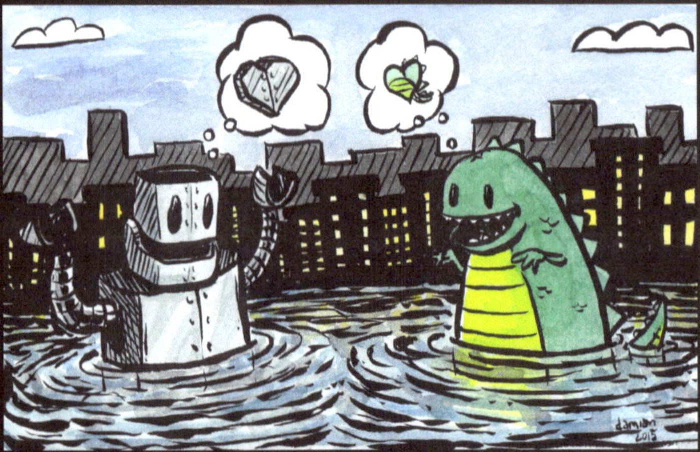
damian 2015

"welcome home!"

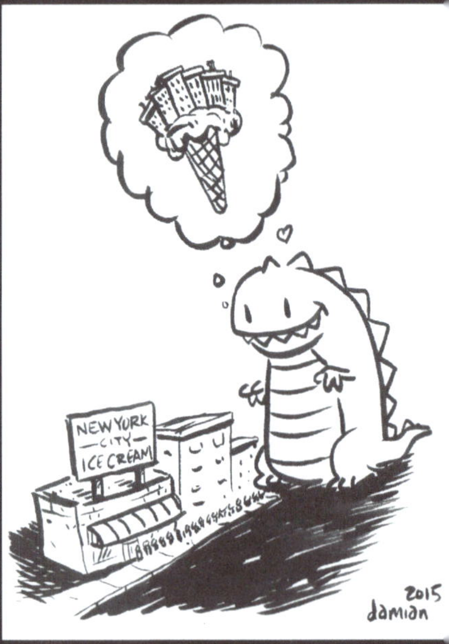
NEW YORK CITY ICE CREAM
2015 damian

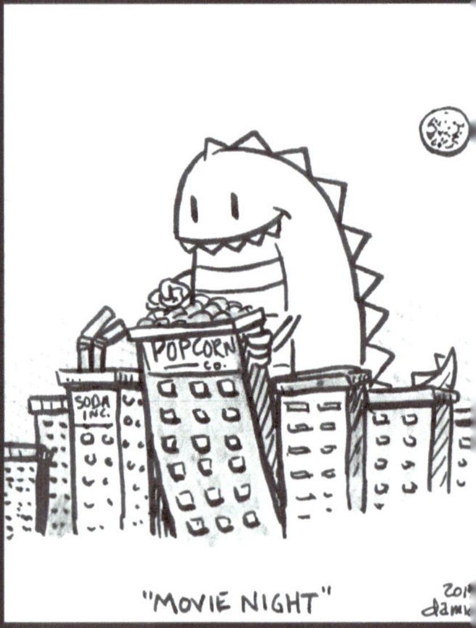
POPCORN CO.
SODA INC.
"MOVIE NIGHT"

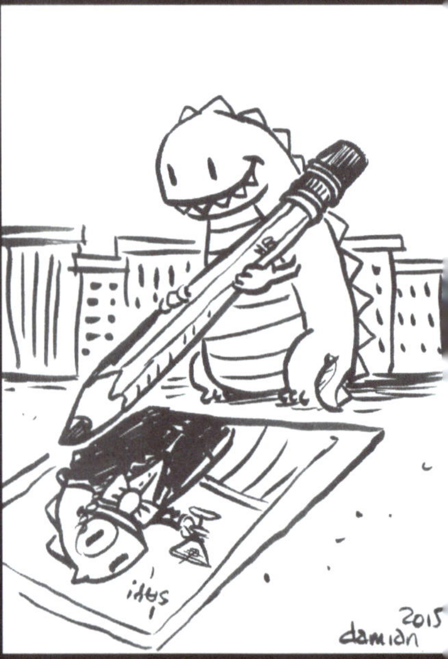
2015 damian

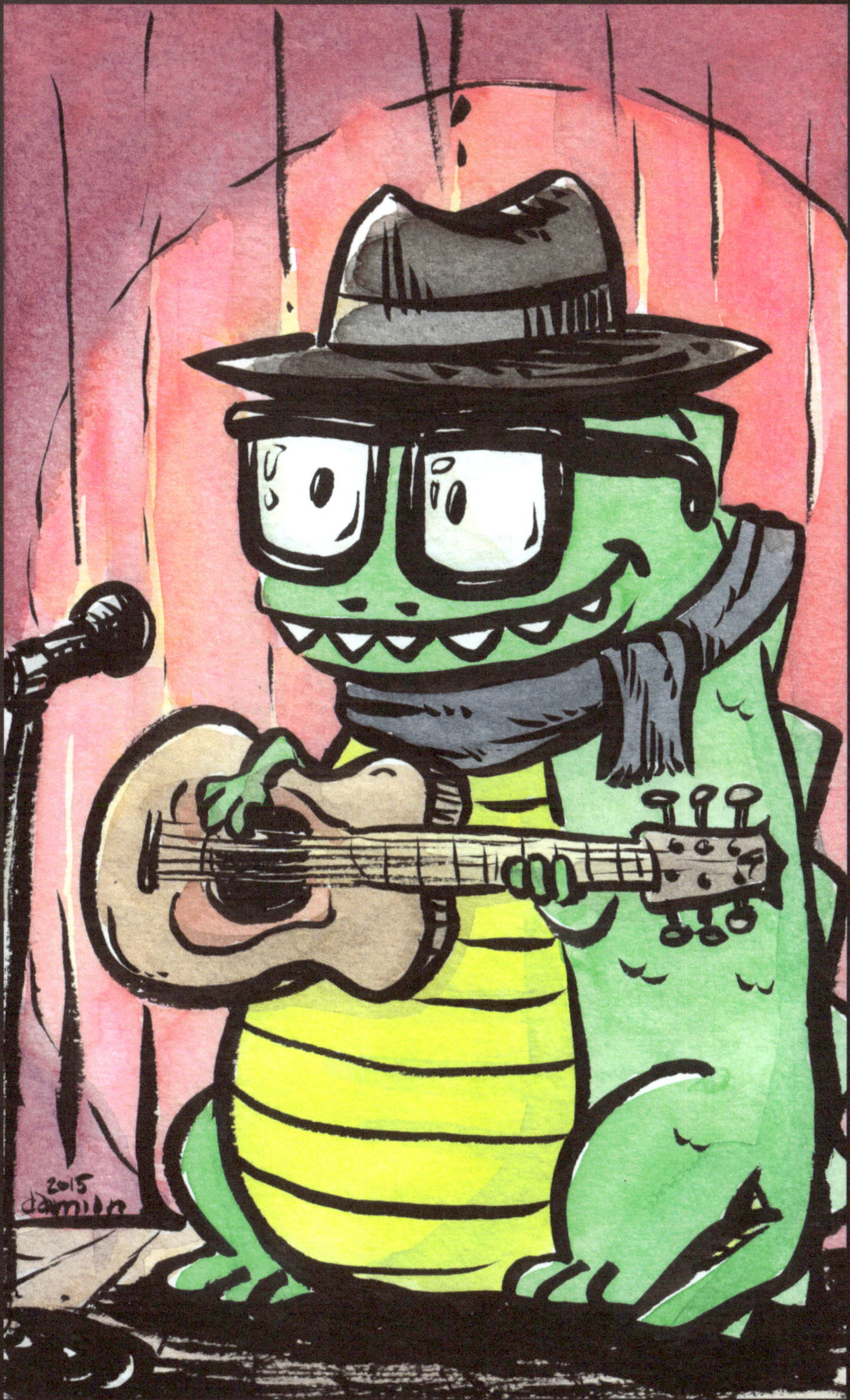
2015
damion

"Elvis Godzillo"

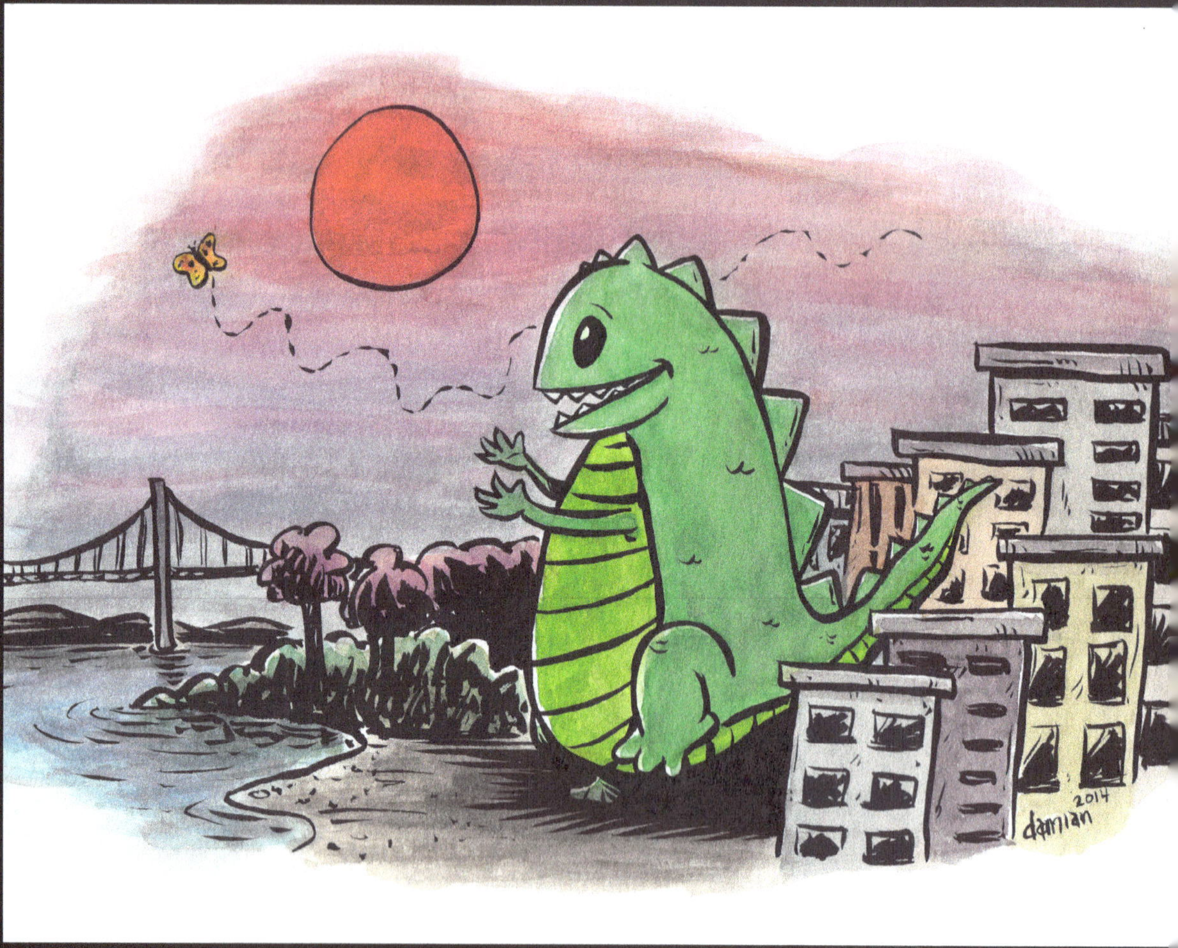
2014
damian

"The Butterfly That Saved Tokyo"

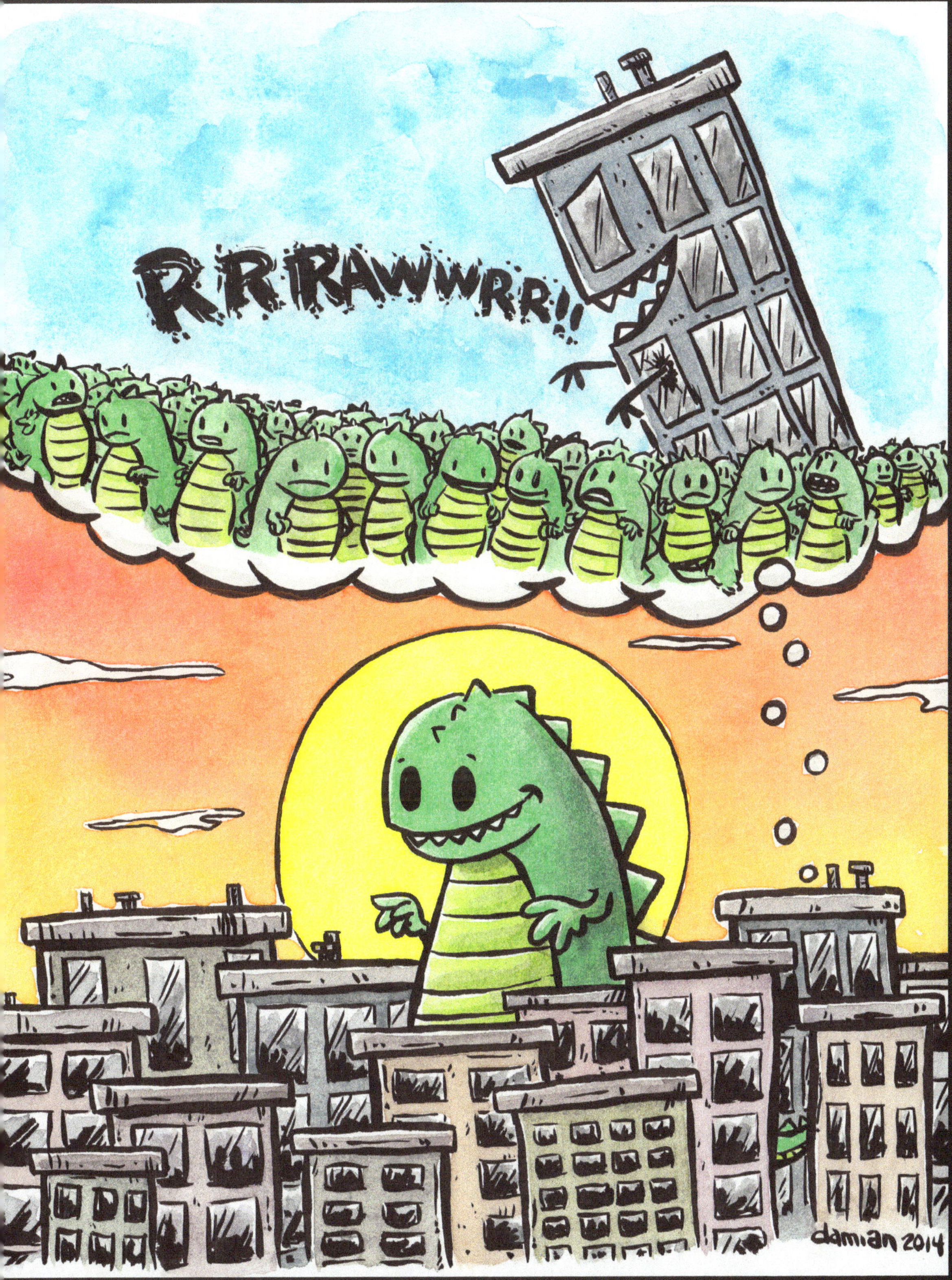
RRRAWWRR!!
damian 2014

"Big Dreams in Little Tokyo"

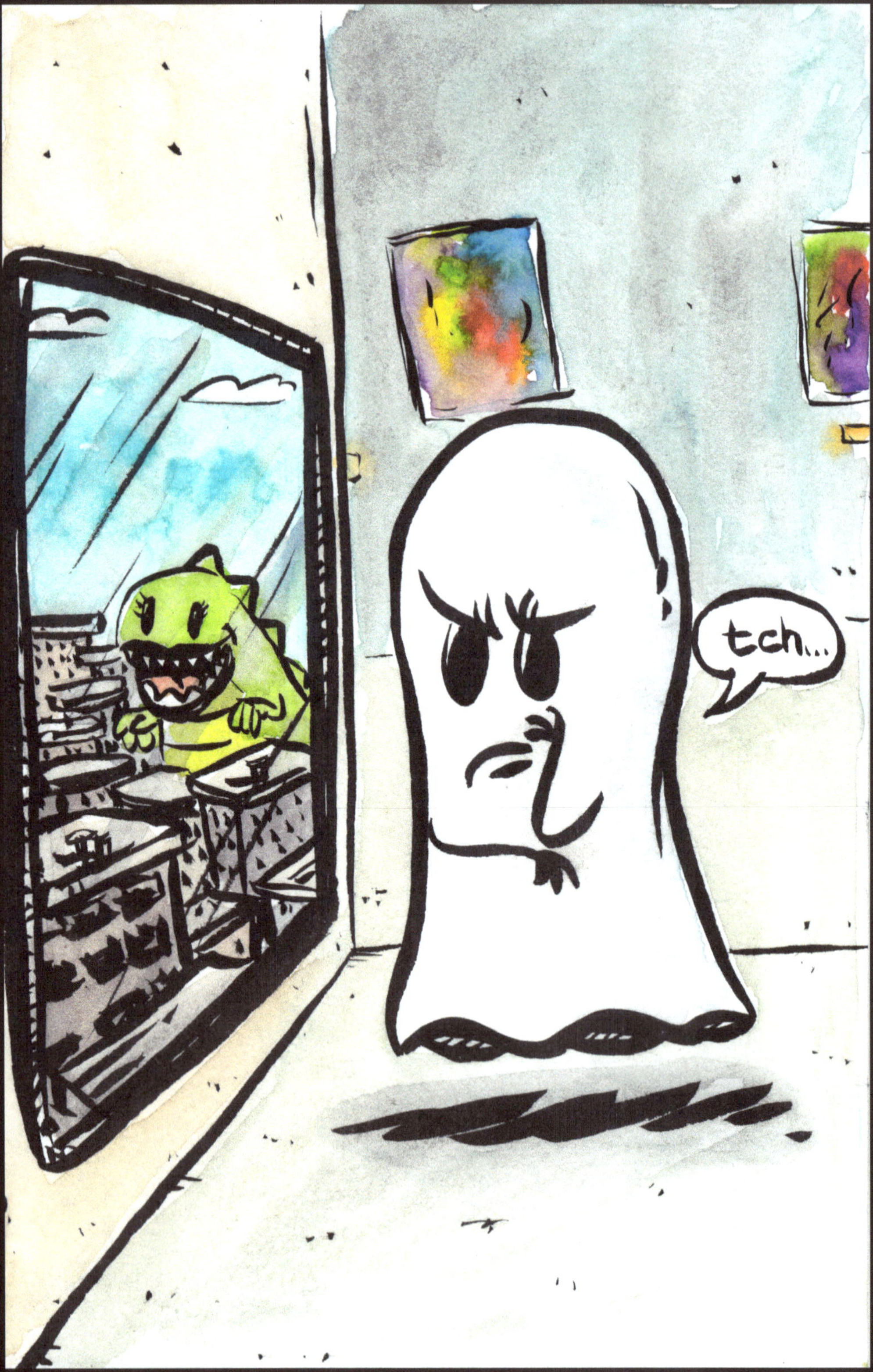
tch...

a drawing entitled "unimpressed ghost mistakes window for modern art"

who's afraid of
GHOSTS?

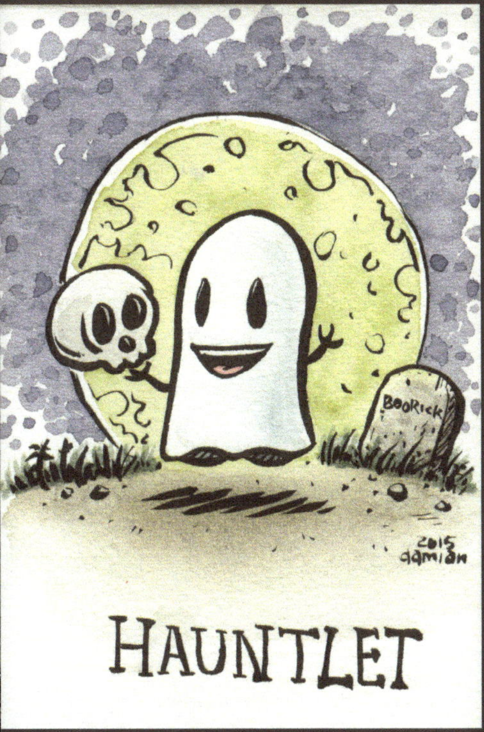
BOORICK
2015
damian
HAUNTLET

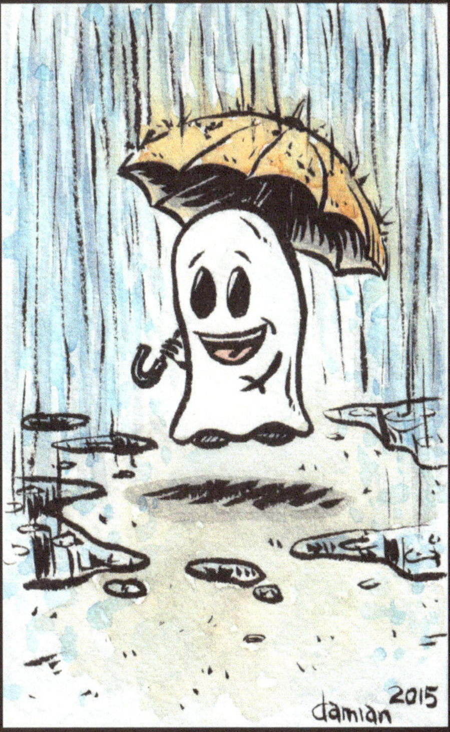
damian 2015

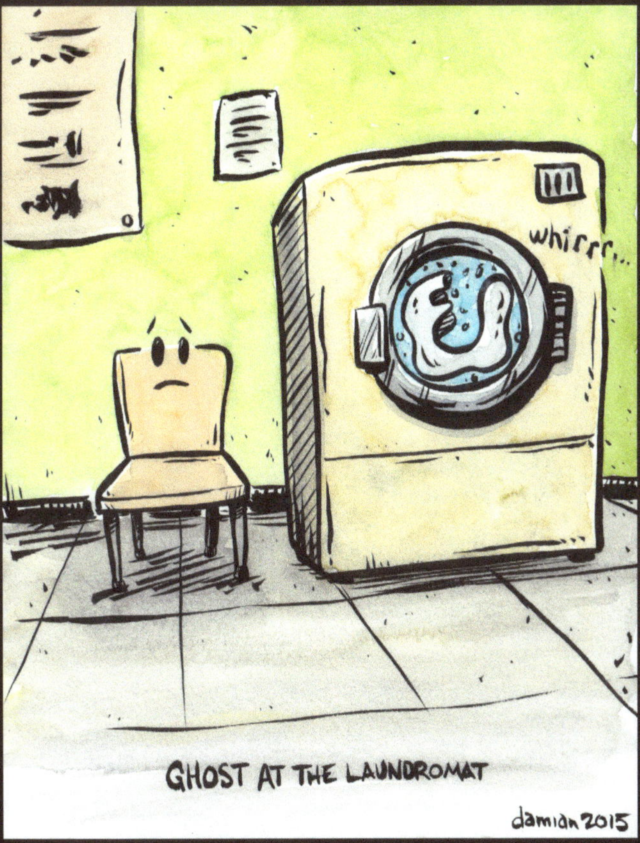
whirrr...
GHOST AT THE LAUNDROMAT
damian 2015

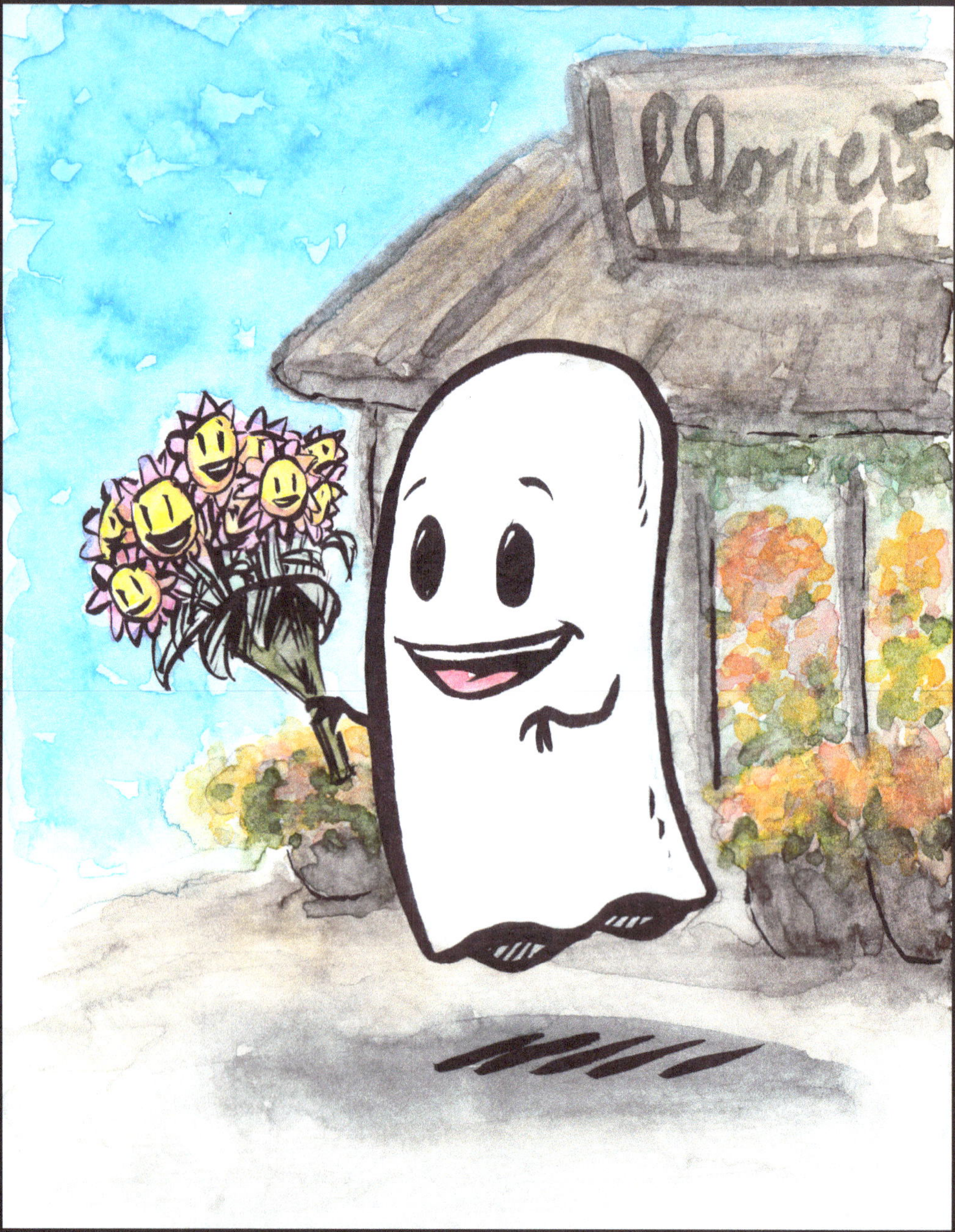
flowers

"boo-kay"

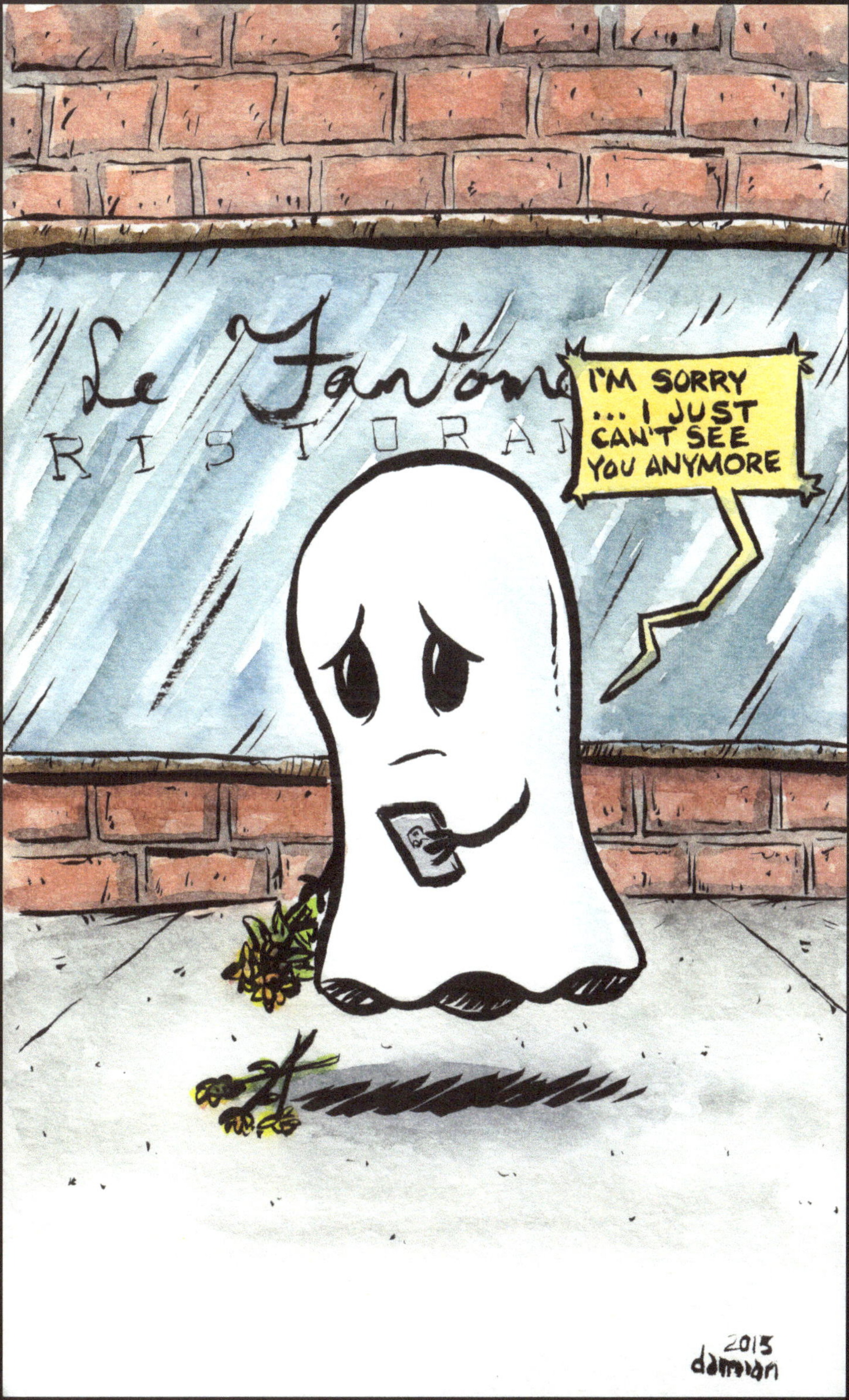
Le Fantome
RISTORAN
I'M SORRY ... I JUST CAN'T SEE YOU ANYMORE
2015 damian

"ghoul problems"

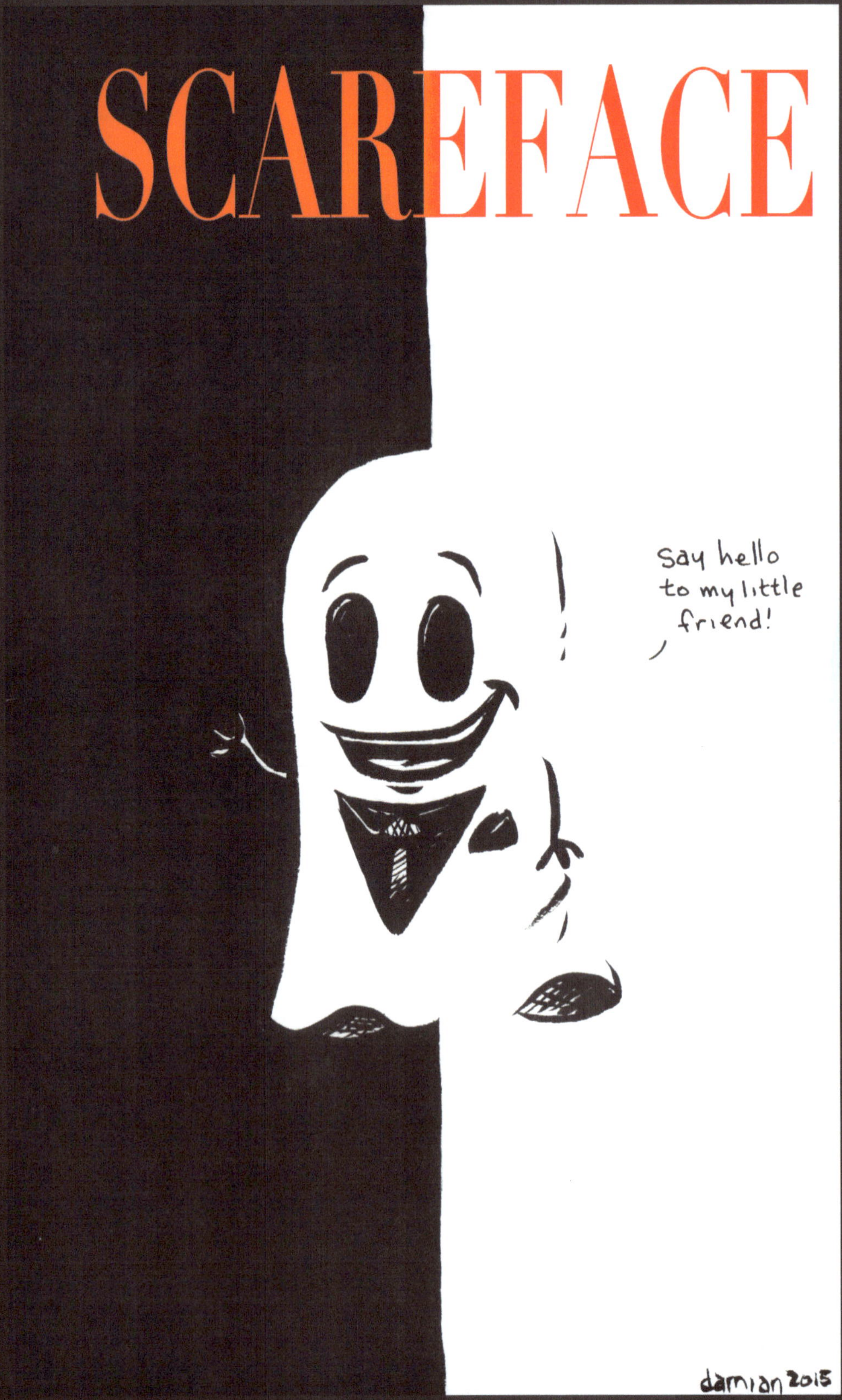
SCAREFACE
say hello to my little friend!
damian 2015

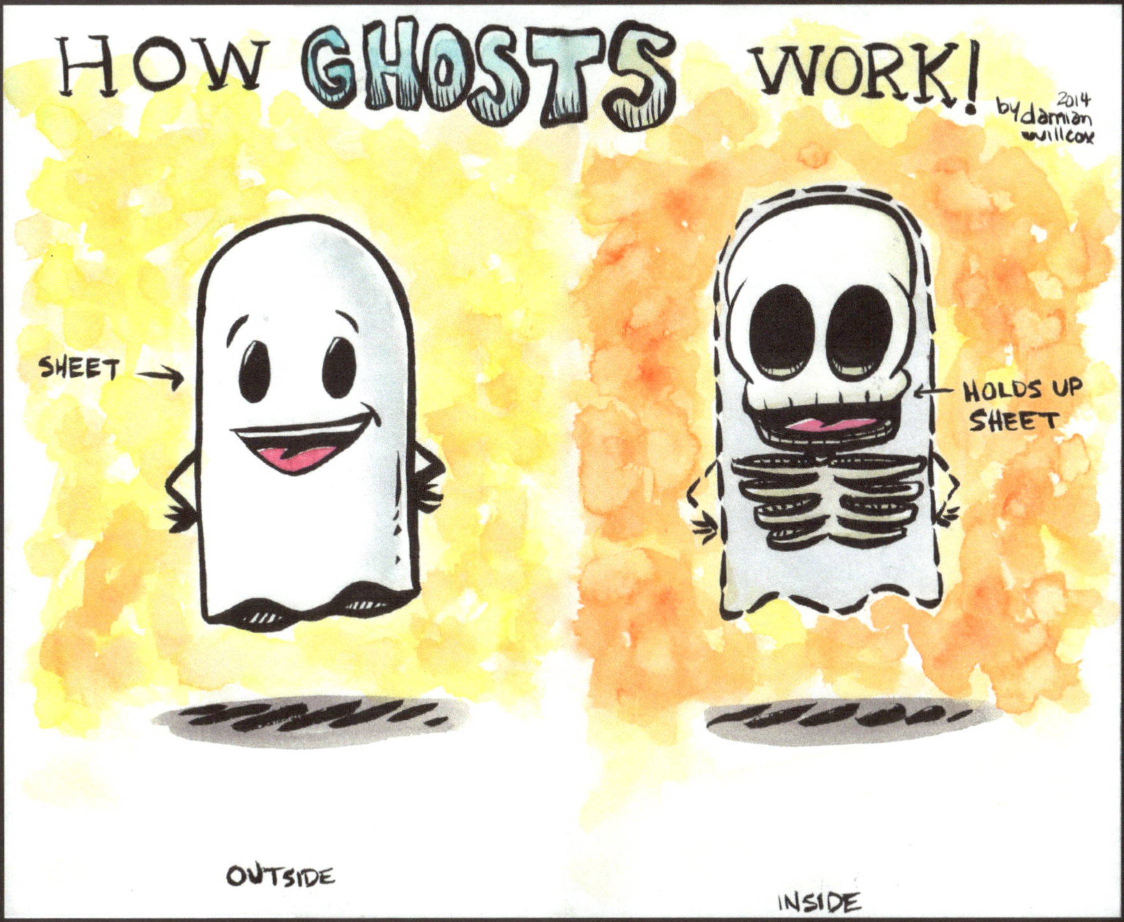
HOW GHOSTS WORK!
2014
by damian willcox
SHEET
HOLDS UP SHEET
OUTSIDE
INSIDE

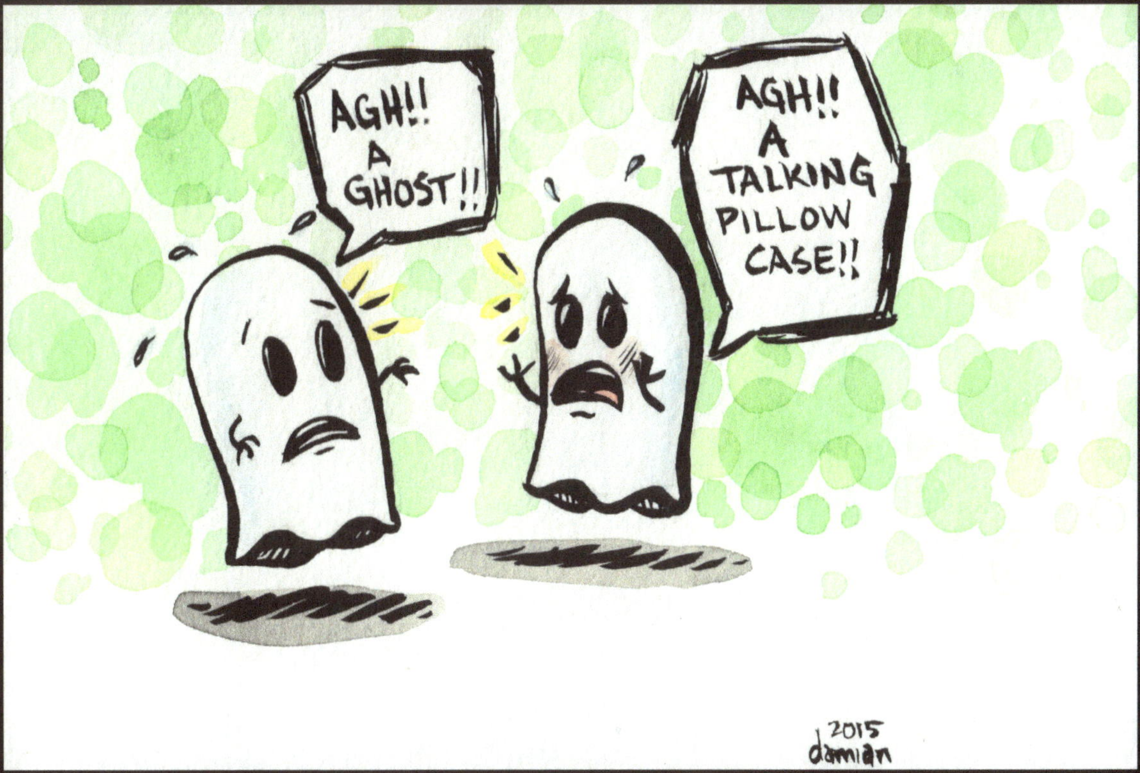
AGH!! A GHOST!!
AGH!! A TALKING PILLOW CASE!!
2015
damian

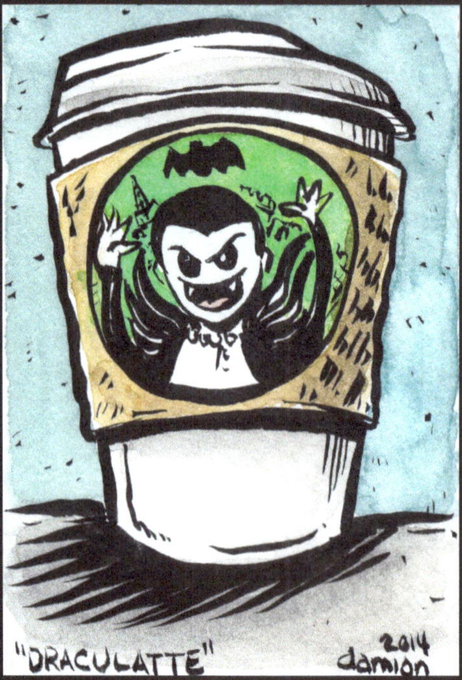
"DRACULATTE"
2014
damian

"Draculatte"

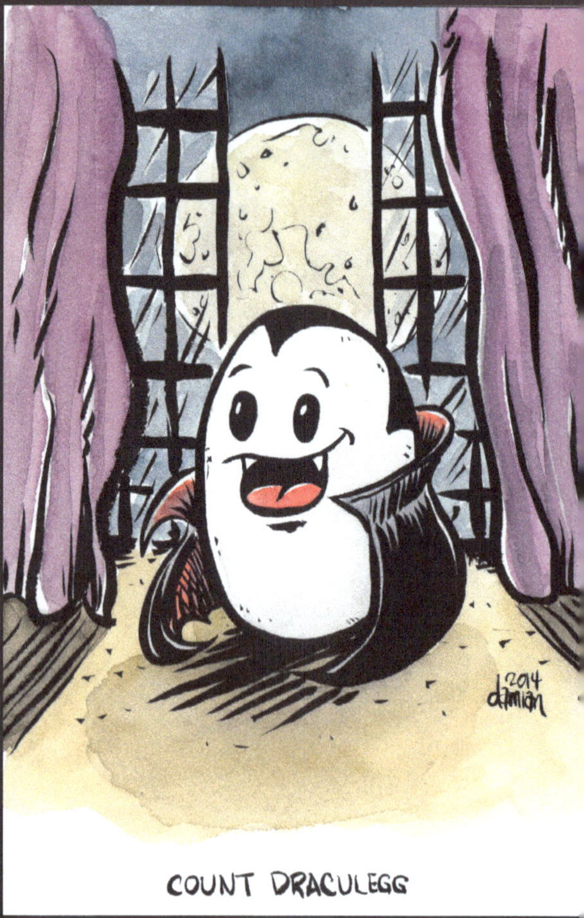
2014
damian
COUNT DRACULEGG

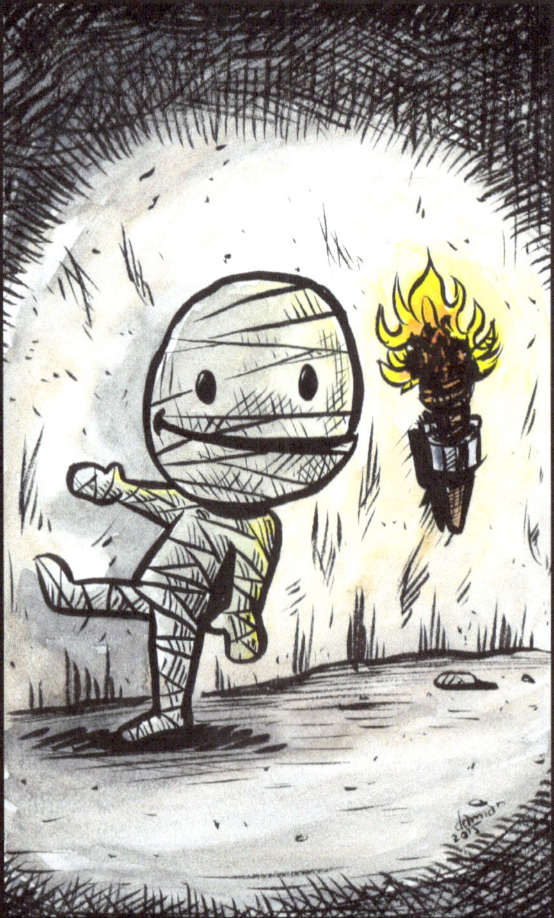

"Zombee"

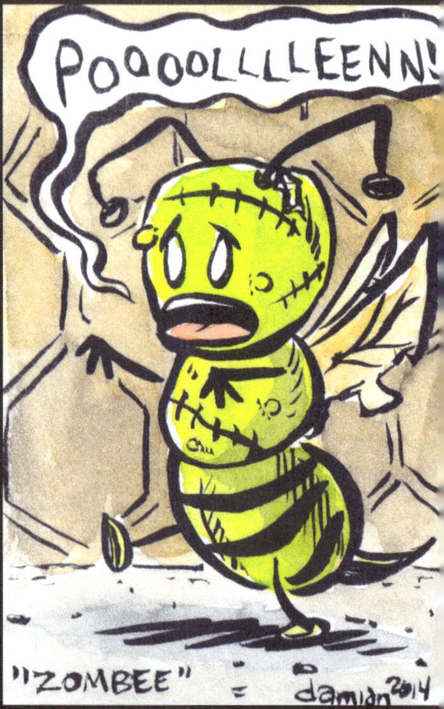
POOOOLLLLLEENN!
"ZOMBEE"
damian 2014

...and other pieces from my SKETCHBOOK

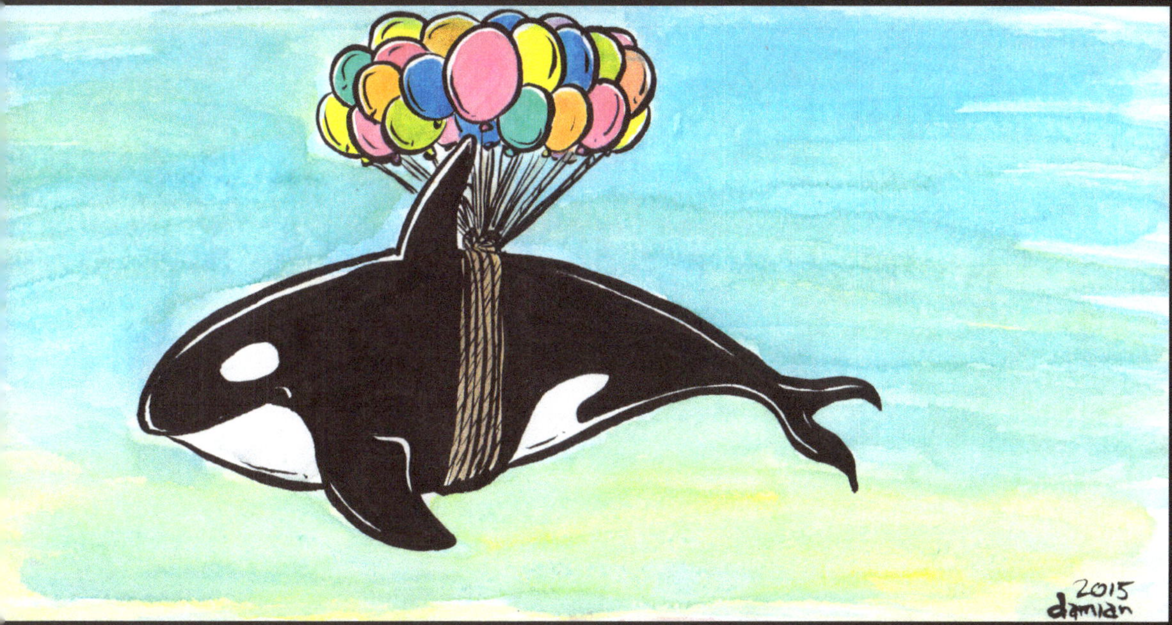
2015
damian

"More like 'Sea-ya' World!"

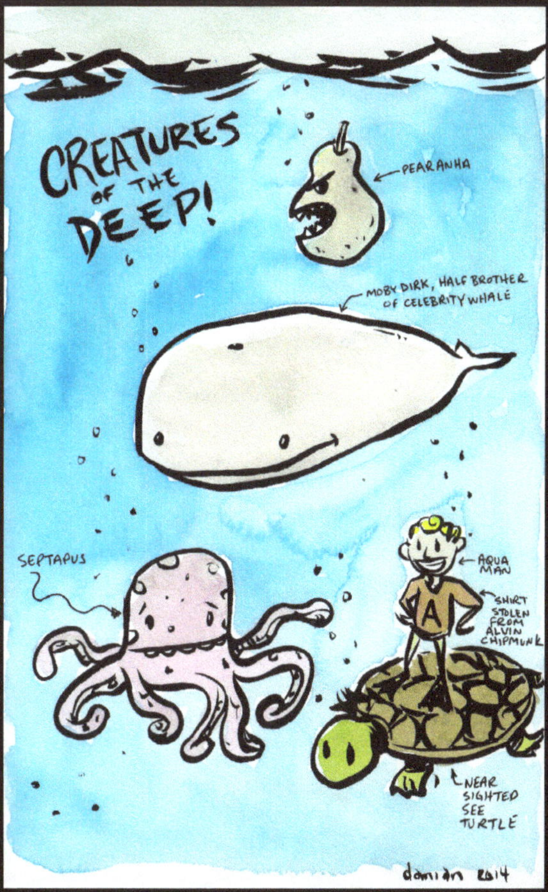
CREATURES OF THE DEEP!
PEARANHA
MOBY DIRK, HALF BROTHER OF CELEBRITY WHALE
SEPTAPUS
AQUA MAN
SHIRT STOLEN FROM ALVIN CHIPMUNK
NEAR SIGHTED SEE TURTLE
damian 2014

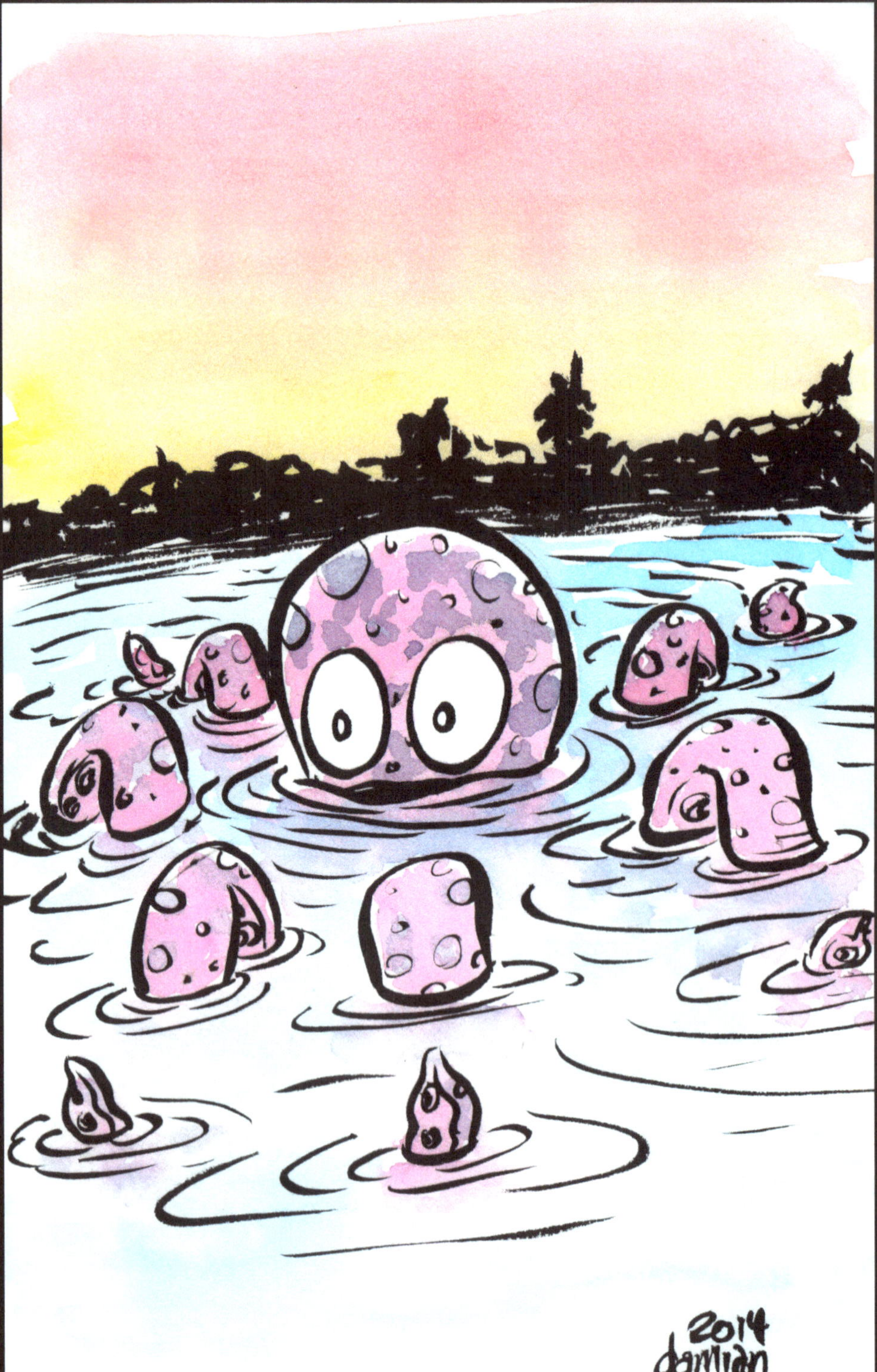
2014
damian

"treading water"

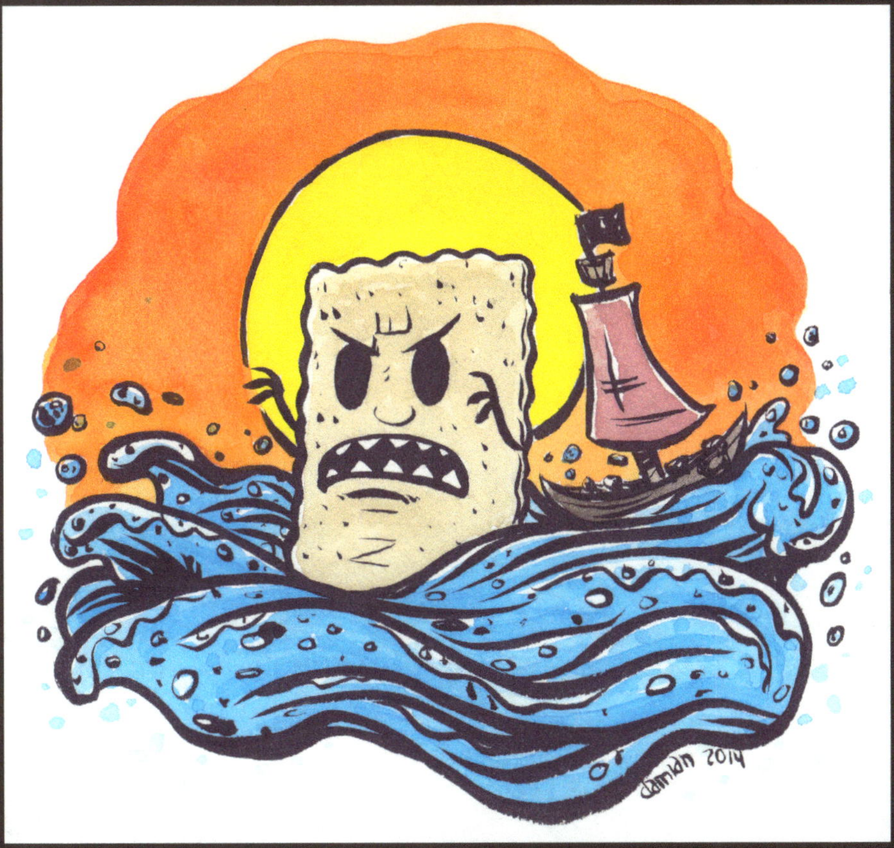
damian 2014

"The terrifyingly true story of the real Sea Biscuit"

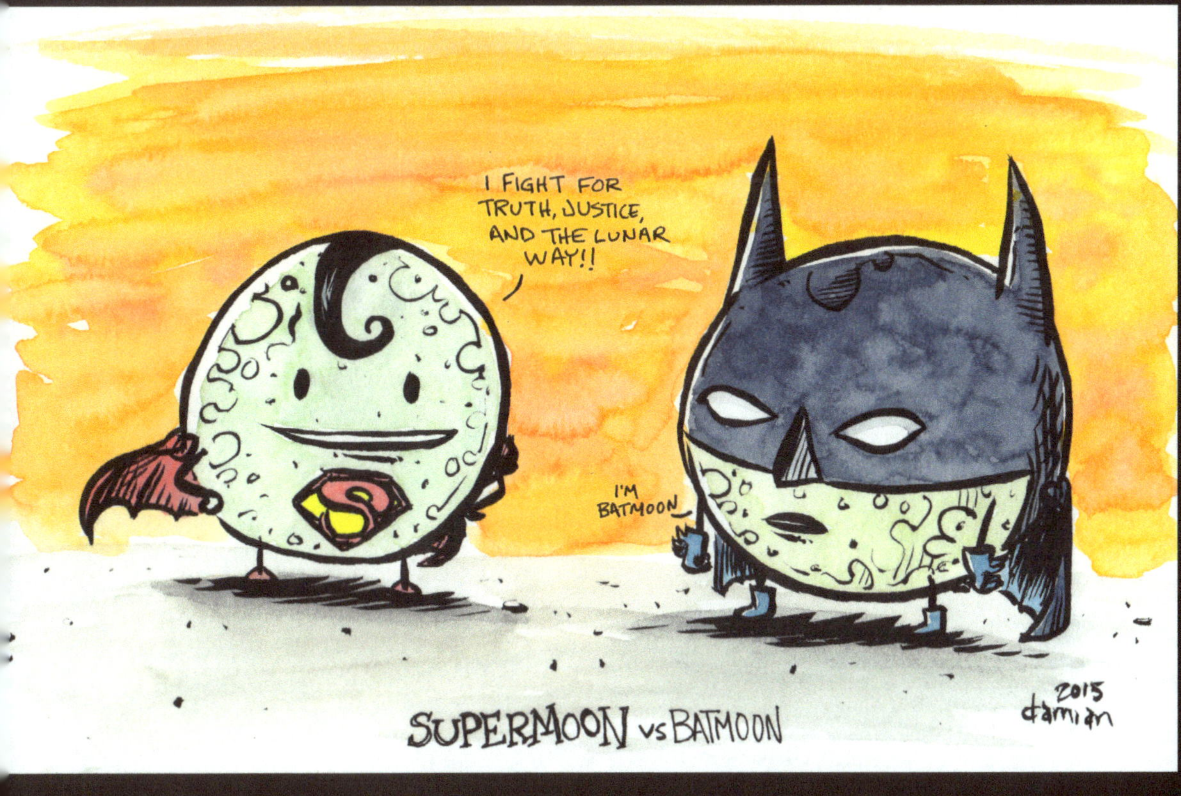
I FIGHT FOR TRUTH, JUSTICE, AND THE LUNAR WAY!!
I'M BATMOON
SUPERMOON vs BATMOON
2015 damian

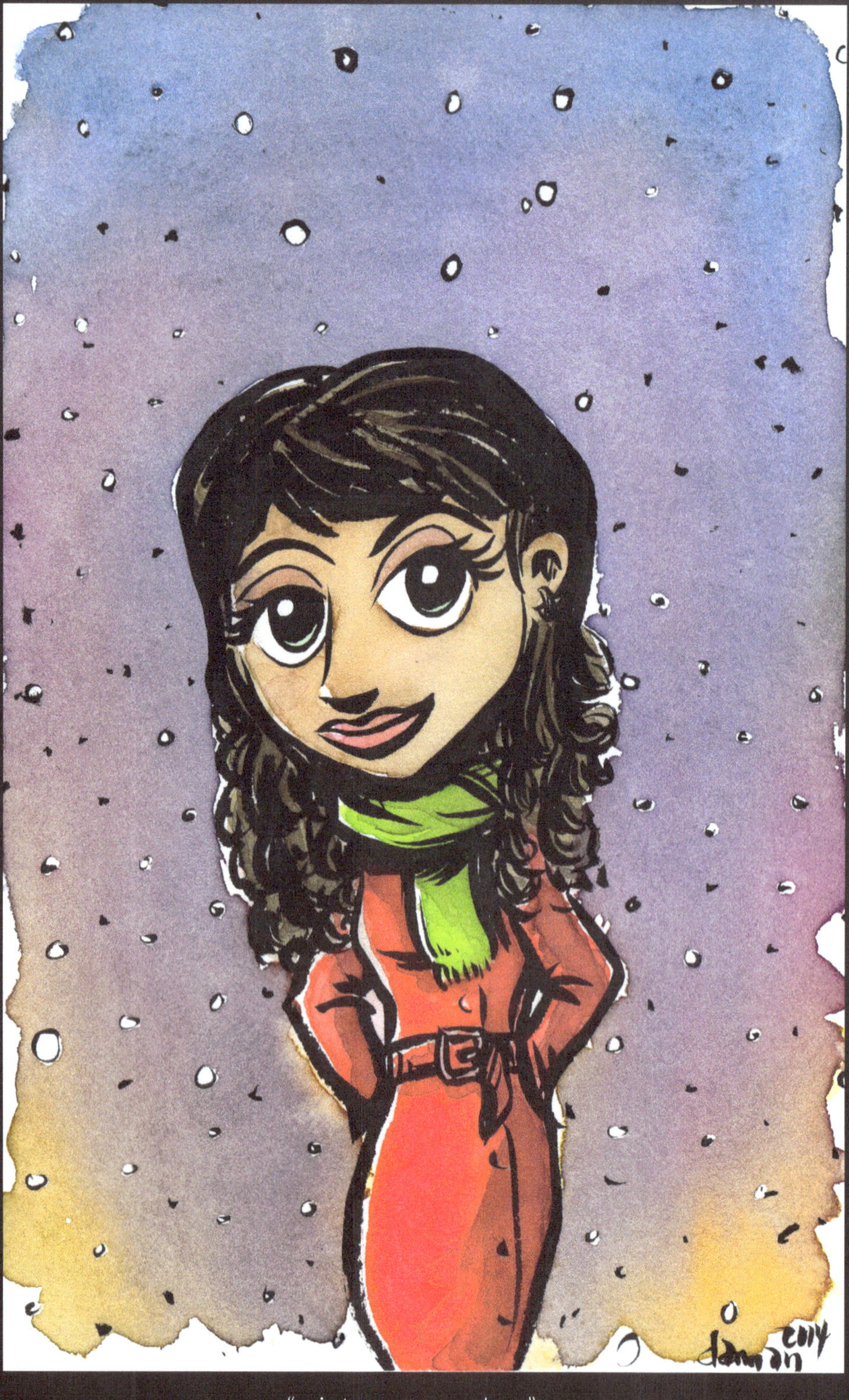

"winter approaches"

about the artist...

damian willcox is an award nominated cartoonist that has been publishing his comics and artwork both in print and online for over twenty years.

During that time he has also written the Too Much Coffee Man Opera with Shannon Wheeler, survived his comics getting TV series related interest from Hollywood types, and has even appeared in a National Chinese television show as a 'wealthy foreigner'.

He currently lives in Calgary, Alberta, Canada and spends his days with his wonderful wife Miyuki and nutty dogs Lychee & Kiwi ("the fruits").

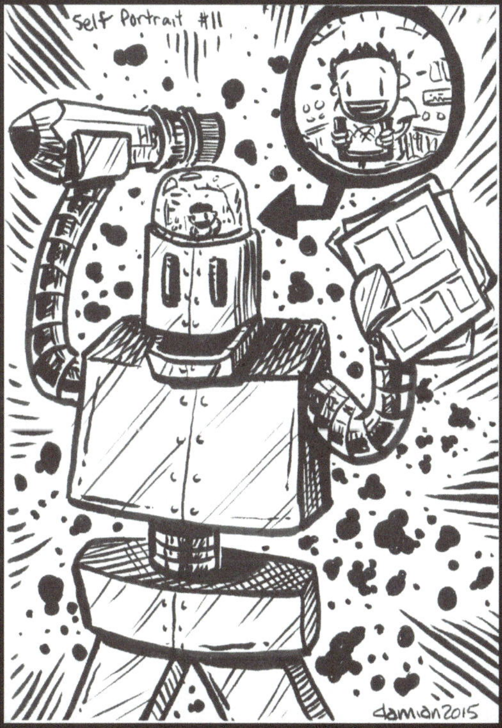
Self Portrait #11
damian2015

thanks for reading!

your comic friend,

damian

tw @dorkboycomics
fb facebook.com/damiandraws
ig instagram.com/dorkboycomics

damian@dorkboycomics.com
dorkboycomics.com

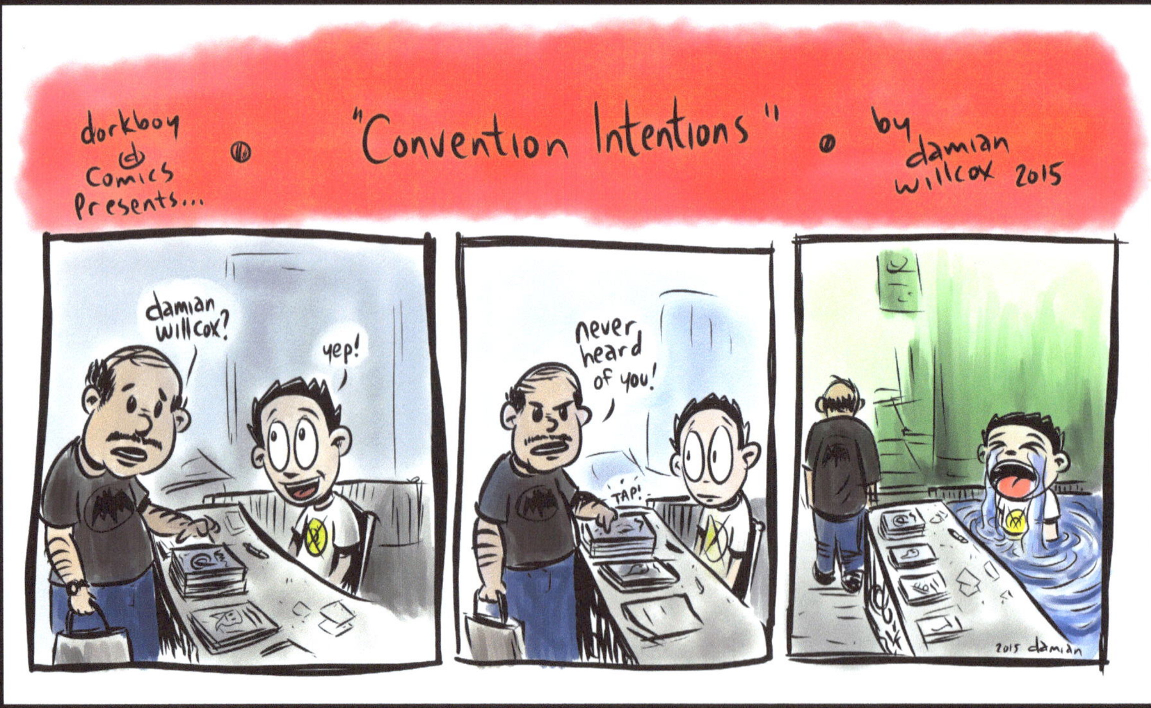
dorkboy comics presents...
"Convention Intentions"
by damian willcox 2015
damian willcox?
yep!
never heard of you!
TAP!
2015 damian

Thanks for picking up my book! I hope you enjoyed reading it as much as I enjoyed making it! See you soon.

damian

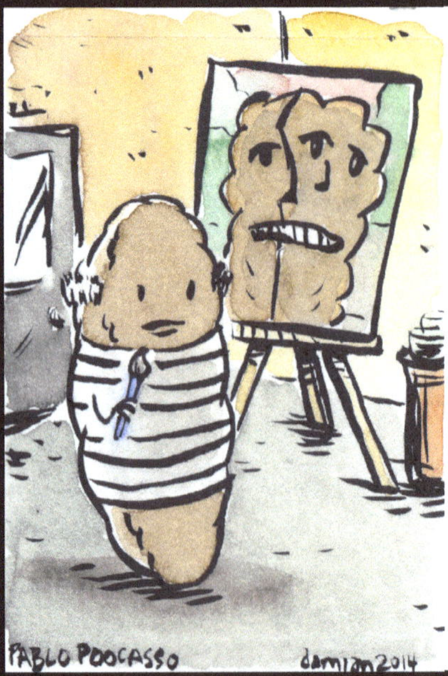
PABLO POOCASSO
damian 2014
"Pablo Poocasso"

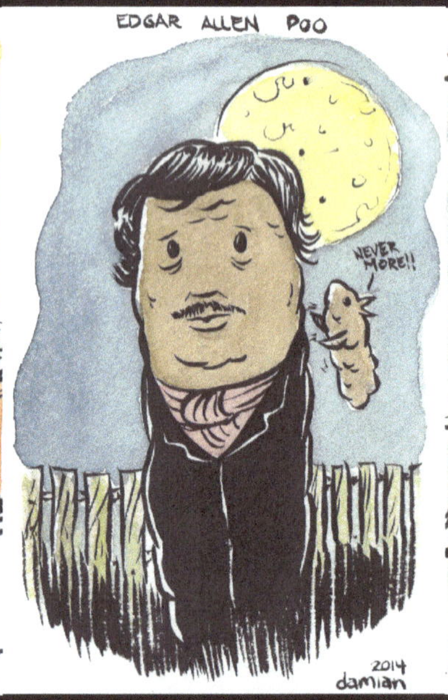
EDGAR ALLEN POO
NEVER MORE!!
2014
damian
"Edgar Allen Poo"

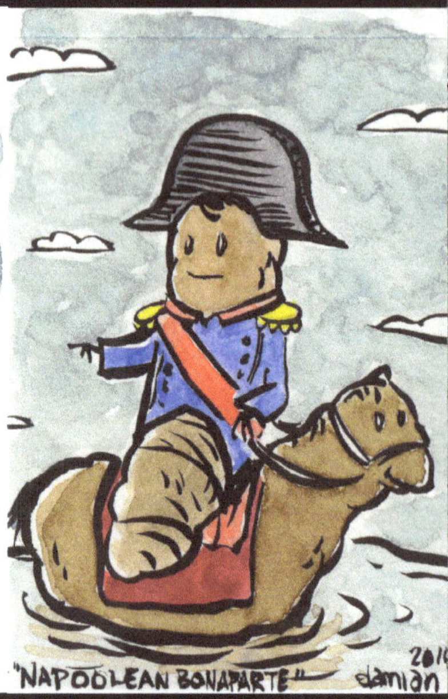
"NAPOOLEAN BONAPARTE"
damian
"Napoolean Bonaparte"